Field Notes *from a* Fungi Forager

Field Notes *from a* Fungi Forager

An Illustrated Journey through the World of
PACIFIC NORTHWEST MUSHROOMS

ASHLEY RODRIGUEZ

With illustrations by Libby England

SASQUATCH BOOKS
SEATTLE

This book is for the fungi.
Thanks for sharing this world with us.

Contents

Land Acknowledgment

THIS BOOK WAS WRITTEN ON THE TRADITIONAL LAND of the shared territory of the modern day Duwamish, Muckleshoot, Snoqualmie, and Suquamish tribes. I want to express gratitude for their stewardship of this territory for countless generations, recognize the ongoing importance of their cultural contributions, and strive to honor their continued connection and presence on this land.

A Cautionary Note

THIS BOOK IS NOT A FIELD GUIDE and should not be used by readers to identify mushroom species, especially ones you plan on eating. Accurately identifying mushroom species is essential in foraging and takes many years of fieldwork and studying field guides. There are many toxic look-alike mushrooms that are not mentioned in this book. The author and publisher make no representations regarding the safety of foraging or consuming wild mushrooms and specifically disclaim any responsibility for any misidentification of mushroom species or certain species' medicinal properties or any health problems or loss resulting from the ingestion of mushrooms or the use of any information contained in this book. Persons who consume mushrooms or other potentially dangerous fungi do so at their own peril and risk illness and even death. Consuming mushrooms of unknown origin should be avoided, and even some mushrooms that are nontoxic for most people may make some people ill.

Introduction

*I contend that the planet's health actually
depends on our respect for fungi.*

–PAUL STAMETS, *MYCELIUM RUNNING*

AS A CHILD GROWING UP in the Pacific Northwest with
conifer-studded woodlands as my backyard, I spent hours
creating worlds out of decaying logs, snacking on tart red
huckleberries, picking wildflowers—and avoiding mushrooms. There was very little motivation to befriend the
fungi. I was terrified they could kill me, and when they
did appear on my dinner plate I was grossed out by their
slimy presence.

Fast-forward a couple of decades and now I'm loud
and proud about my fungi fandom. There were many
encounters along the way that led to this dramatic shift
in my relationship with mushrooms, some of which you'll
read about in the following pages. The thing about fear is
that with knowledge, curiosity, and listening, it can trans-
form into wonder and awe. Once I started to understand
fungi more, my appreciation of them exploded. It began
as a desire to enjoy eating them. As a chef and recipe
developer, I wanted to expand my palate and overcome

my aversion to mushrooms, so I started to add them to dishes, first by chopping them up very finely so I wasn't overwhelmed by the texture and instead could focus on the earthy, umami-rich flavor. Eating wild mushrooms was a much different experience than dodging the button mushrooms from my childhood. I went from avoiding mushrooms to spending hours and hours in the woods trying to find them. Now, I delight in seeing any and all mushrooms (not just the edible ones). A walk in the woods with me means that our conversation will always be interrupted by mushroom sightings.

That is essentially the premise and purpose of this book: to share my knowledge and love of the fungal world so that mushrooms can get the appreciation they rightly deserve. I'm honored to be your co-guide, along with the fungi, on this journey. I am a passionate forager and have been for many years. I have had the distinct pleasure of being guided by some of the best and most knowledgeable mushroom experts in the field. I'm also a nature-therapy and eco-spiritual guide, and I've been working in the food world for over two decades. Initially, I came to love foraging for the incredible ingredients the woods could provide, but the more I learn, the more I appreciate fungi for the inherent wisdom, beauty, medicine, and healing they provide to the entire ecosystem.

THIS IS NOT A FORAGING guide. It's not meant to be a scientific tome used for proper identification in the field. There are many incredible resources out there for that (my recommendations are listed on page 155). Rather, this is for the open-minded ones who are eager to learn a little bit about the hidden knowledge that fungi possess and their role in the interconnection of life, all centered in the beautiful and fertile ground of the Pacific Northwest.

Our journey through the world of fungi aims to dispel misconceptions and replace them with delight, awe, wonder, and a little bit of whimsy.

We'll begin by learning more about how fungi function and interact with the natural world, including ourselves. We'll touch on current research about how mushrooms are helping to save the planet and our mental health. We'll look at the ecosystems and ecology of the Pacific Northwest and its lush and welcoming habitat for many species. Next, we'll cover best practices for foraging or simply going out for a mushroom appreciation hike or wander.

The bulk of the book is a collection of field notes from the forest floor: an exploration of the many different types of mushrooms that call this special region home, from the famous *Morchella* (morel, pages 102–107) and *Cantharellus* (chanterelle, pages 44–49) to the lesser-known species that are equally fascinating, like the bluish-purple *Lepista nuda* (wood blewit, page 92) and *Hydnellum peckii* (bleeding tooth fungus, page 80), which oozes brilliant red droplets. Here, we'll befriend each of these mushrooms by getting to know their appearance and what distinguishes them from other species, and we'll look at how some of them have been used throughout different cultures and in stories or myths.

This book is an ode to the fungi among us, a celebration of the natural world and the magic that can be found in even the smallest beings. Through the lens of these humble fungi, we'll explore the interconnectedness of all living things and gain a deeper appreciation for the beauty and complexity of our bioregion. Whether you're a seasoned forager or just starting to appreciate the beauty of mushrooms, there's something in these pages for everyone. Allow the scent of damp earth and the sight of vibrant caps, hidden mycelial webs, and puffs of smokelike spores be our guide.

The Future of Fungi

Today, more than 90% of all plant species depend on mycorrhizal fungi. They are the rule, not the exception. . . . Out of this intimate partnership . . . plants and mycorrhizal fungi enact a collective flourishing that underpins our past, present and future. We are unthinking without them, yet seldom do we think about them. The cost of our neglect has never been more apparent. It is an attitude we can't afford to sustain.

—MERLIN SHELDRAKE, *ENTANGLED LIFE*

SO OFTEN THE DESIRE TO get to know fungi is to be able to identify a few of their most delicious species. I'll admit, that's how I was pulled in. People are naturally drawn to the ones they can eat, so we begin by learning how to recognize a few specific mushroom varieties. Along the way, you meet mycelium and immerse yourself in the intricate world of hypha threads in the soil.

As you explore this hidden realm, the fungi gently encourage you to broaden your perspective. They invite you to lift your head from the ground and take in the bigger picture. Look around at the trees near the porcini you just plucked, notice other plant species growing alongside the chanterelle, and listen to the birdsong when morel mushrooms start popping up. The fungi teach us how we're all connected.

Fewer than 5 percent of fungi species have been identified and yet what we do know is enough to blow your mind. For thousands of years, humans have found many ways to use fungi as food, fermenting agents, materials, medicines, and pathways into deeper spiritual connection. The recent scientific studies of mushrooms are truly astounding. We now know that through the mycelial web, nutrients are being passed under the forest floor in order to preserve and protect the ecosystem, commonly referred to as the "wood wide web." (But not all mushrooms are friendly with the trees; some—like the *Armillaria ostoyae* on page 33, which causes root disease—have the ability to decimate entire forests.) Mushrooms have emerged as a new material for use in the fashion industry, which presently contributes to 8–10 percent of global emissions, according to the United Nations. The utilization of fungi, particularly their mycelium, has allowed for the development of sustainable materials that resemble leather. Mushrooms also possess a remarkable capability to decompose hazardous waste and plastics. Oyster mushrooms (pages 121–123), for instance, have proven highly effective in eliminating pesticides and heavy metals from polluted sites, indicating that fungi could serve as invaluable tools in restoring ecological balance. Additionally, mushrooms may play a crucial role in promoting both our mental and physical well-being. Research indicates that fungi have exhibited potential in aiding the recovery and prevention of certain cancers. Recent studies on psychedelic mushrooms have revealed that patients who consume these mushrooms have experienced improvements in mental health conditions such as anxiety and depression.

Now, more than ever, we need the fungi. Getting to know them and their environments, and learning how we can best be in relationship with them, might be one of the most important things we can do for our planet and one another.

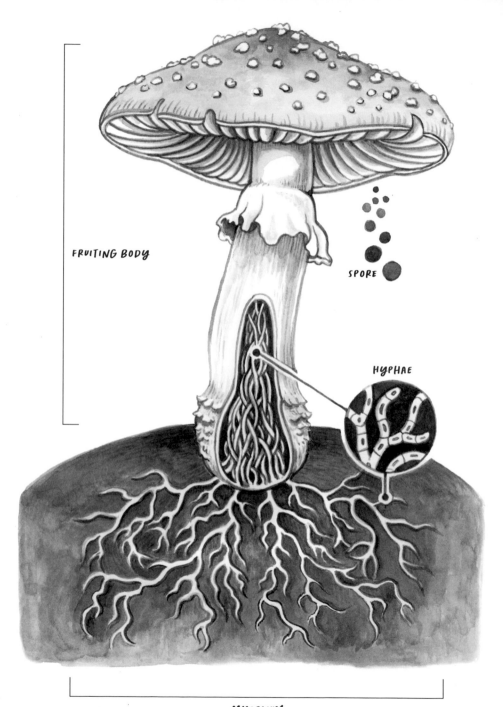

FRUITING BODY

SPORE

HYPHAE

MYCELIUM

On Mushrooms

Mushrooms were the window by which I came to understand nature in a deeper way.

—EUGENIA BONE, *FANTASTIC FUNGI*

FUNGI ARE ORGANISMS THAT LACK chlorophyll, leaves, true stems, and roots. They aren't quite plants and are not animals but belong in their own kingdom: the kingdom of fungi. In fact, we are more closely related to fungi than they are to plants.

Mushrooms are the fruiting body of fungi, although not all fungi grow mushrooms. (Mushrooms are only a small part of the whole that make up a fungus.) These fruiting bodies grow aboveground, on soil, trees, dead logs, twigs, stumps, or even on insects, depending on the species. One of the jobs of the mushroom is to aid in spore dispersal, which is the reproductive action of fungi. Spores are released in a variety of ways and often require the help of rain, flies, grazing animals, or humans to help spread them. Spores are like the seeds of the fungi, and each fruiting body can contain billions of spores.

The main body of the fungus is the mycelium, which is like an underground web of threadlike hyphae used to break down and absorb nutrients and water for the fungus. It can also connect to the surrounding trees and plants, creating a path of reciprocity. Next time you are outside, or even near one of your houseplants, pick up a bit of the soil and notice all the white webbing found in the dirt; that's mycelium! In healthy soil you can find up to eight miles of mycelium in one cubic inch of dirt.

Fungi are heterotrophic, meaning that they get all they need to live from other organisms rather than making their own food, like plants do. The massive world of fungi is organized into four different groups based on how they do this:

Saprotrophic

These fungi derive their nutrients from decaying organic matter. They are essential to cleaning our forests by speeding up the decomposition process, turning dead trees, wood, leaf litter, animal remains, and waste into nutrient-rich soil.

Mycorrhizal

In this category, the fungi form a relationship with a living plant, most often a tree, that is beneficial for both. The mycelium of mycorrhizal mushrooms acts as a transportation system, gathering and passing along necessary nutrients. The fungi receive sugar produced by the plants through photosynthesis, while the plant receives nitrogen and phosphorus that the mushroom has gathered from the soil through the hyphae. About one-third of all mushrooms are mycorrhizal. In his book *Entangled Life*, Merlin Sheldrake states that over 90 percent of all plant species depend on mycorrhizal fungi.

Parasitic   Fungi in this category receive nutrients from a plant or animal but do not return the favor, eventually killing their host. Sometimes it is hard to distinguish between parasites and saprotrophs as they both live off already-weakened hosts. Most fungi in this category do not produce mushrooms and are too small to be seen or noticed.

Endophytic   This category is mainly made up of small fungi that colonize a plant but don't do any damage. In fact, the host plant is likely to benefit from the "invasion" by receiving more nutrients and the ability to resist pathogens. Research shows that most plants contain endophytic fungi, which are found in plant leaves, stems, flowers, and seeds (unlike mycorrhizal fungi, which are found in the roots).

MUSHROOM ANATOMY

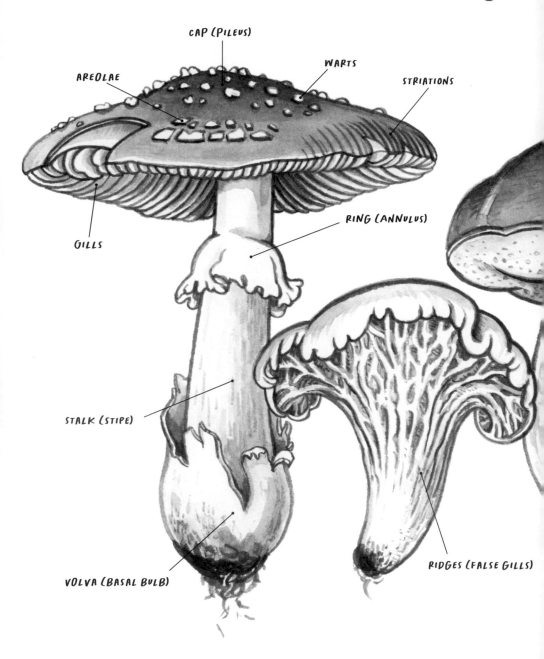

CAP (PILEUS)

WARTS

AREOLAE

STRIATIONS

GILLS

RING (ANNULUS)

STALK (STIPE)

RIDGES (FALSE GILLS)

VOLVA (BASAL BULB)

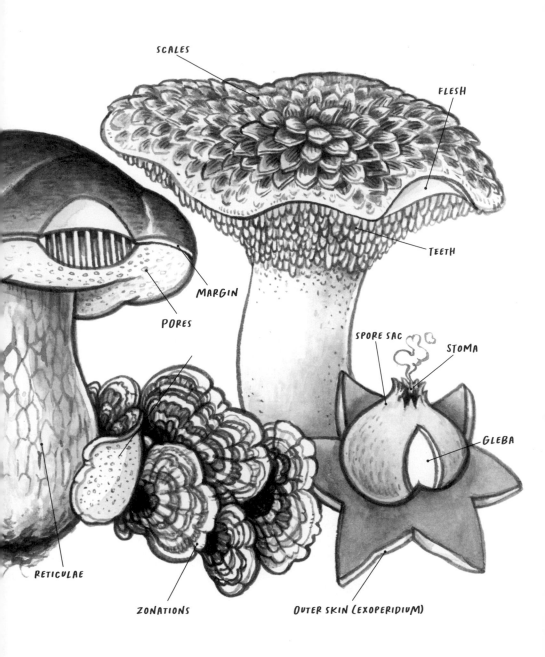

SCALES

FLESH

MARGIN

PORES

TEETH

SPORE SAC

STOMA

GLEBA

RETICULAE

ZONATIONS

OUTER SKIN (EXOPERIDIUM)

See the Glossary on pages 151–153 for more information on terms.

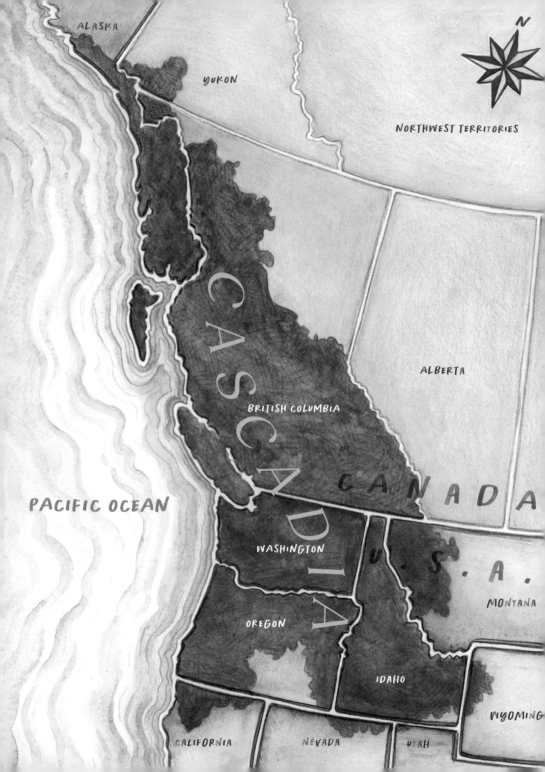

Ecology of the Pacific Northwest

*Look deep into nature, and then you will
understand everything better.*

–ALBERT EINSTEIN to Margo Einstein, 1951; quote by Hanna Loewy
in A&E television's Einstein biography, VPI International, 1991

THE AREA KNOWN AS CASCADIA in the Pacific Northwest
includes Washington, Oregon, Northern California,
coastal Alaska, parts of British Columbia, and Idaho. For
our purposes, we've grouped these regions together as
they all have a similar fungi-growing ecology even though
there are differing ecosystems throughout the region.
Having grown up in the Northwest my entire life, I feel
suited to boast about our vast and varying ecosystems.
The Pacific Northwest is home to many damp, diverse,
and thriving ecosystems where fungi flourish. We live in
a climate where there are distinct seasons: dry summers
and cool, wet falls, winters, and springs. We all are very
aware that rain is a part of life in the Northwest, and
while many see that as a negative aspect of our home, the
mushrooms thrive because of it. Moisture is essential for
the growth and development of many mushrooms. In fact,
most mushrooms are made up of 80–90 percent water,
and thanks to our abundance of rain the mushrooms are
plentiful. Many mushrooms, including the bird's nest
fungi (page 110), use rain as a way of distributing their
spores. This makes the area a mushroom lover's dream.

Coastal rain forests, enveloped in mist, host western red cedar, Sitka spruce, and Douglas fir. Mosses and ferns carpet the forest floor and drip off towering cedar and fir limbs. The balance between land and sea sustains a vibrant ecosystem where salmon journey from rivers to the ocean and back, enriching the forest and its inhabitants. Marine ecosystems thrive along the intricate coastline. Rocky shores and kelp forests support a rich diversity of marine life, including orcas and sea otters.

Inland valleys rise to majestic forests of conifers like Douglas fir and western hemlock. Under their shade, understory plants like sword ferns, trilliums, salal, and huckleberries grow in abundance. Fungi and trees engage in mycorrhizal relationships, with mycelium facilitating nutrient exchange and forests supporting diverse mushroom species much to the delight of insects, animals, and human foragers alike.

As you ascend the Cascade or Olympic mountains, you're rewarded with a stunning expanse of alpine meadows, subalpine forests, and rugged peaks. Hardy species such as mountain goats and pikas have adapted to the harsh alpine conditions, and in these regions I've found porcini (page 38–41), chanterelles (pages 44–49), and the highly prized matsutake (page 143).

The vegetation east of the mountains is predominantly ponderosa pine, red fir, white fir, and lodgepole pine. Even though the east side of the mountains sees less rain, the soil is nourished by the rivers that run like veins. Plenty of mushrooms love the lush lands this side of the mountains, including morels (pages 102–107), porcini (pages 38–41), and many more.

The Pacific Northwest's diverse ecosystems play a vital role in the health of our planet. The forests absorb carbon dioxide, helping to mitigate climate change. Rivers and streams provide spawning grounds for salmon, which enrich both land and aquatic ecosystems. Wetlands and estuaries filter water as it flows from mountains to the sea. All of this creates an ideal habitat for countless fungi species, which then help to sustain the trees, plants, animals, and soil in a reciprocal relationship.

On Foraging

*Give thanks for what you have been given. Give a gift,
in reciprocity for what you have taken. Sustain the
ones who sustain you and the earth will last forever.*

—ROBIN WALL KIMMERER, *BRAIDING SWEETGRASS*

WHILE THIS IS NOT A field guide for foraging, I want to emphasize some best practices because it's highly likely that if you're into mushrooms you'll want to forage (or you already do!).

There is always the option of going on a mushroom "foray," which is a common term used for when you are seeking out the mushrooms in order to understand them better, not harvesting them for food, medicine, art, or other uses. Whatever you call it, I love using mushrooms as the reason to just get outside. Kids and adults (this one especially) alike love the treasure hunt that is looking for mushrooms. It's been extensively researched, and we likely all know from our own experience that spending time outside is one of the best things we can do for our mental, physical, and even spiritual health. It's also, I believe, essential to the care of our planet. When we love the Earth and the particular beings that inhabit the natural world, we work harder to protect her. Spending time in nature does wonders for building that relationship and recognizing that we are all in this together.

If you're planning on collecting mushrooms for the sake of eating them, it's best to first go out with a guide many times to really familiarize yourself with the species you hope to gather.

If you plan to harvest mushrooms for any reason, familiarize yourself with the rules and regulations in your specific area. Gathering mushrooms is restricted and off-limits in many national parks, and other public parks may have a limit or require a permit. The US Forest Service site is a good place to start. My local mycological society (Puget Sound Mycological Society) also has useful information on their site. See Resources on page 155 for more information.

Guidebooks are incredibly helpful and full of great information, but there is nothing better than identifying mushroom species in person. Join a local mycological society and attend their meetings and forays. Never ingest a mushroom unless you are 100 percent certain of its identity. When you try a new species, try a small amount first, wait a few days and if you don't experience a reaction, it's likely fine to eat more.

It's common practice in the mushroom world to not ask about the specific location of where a forager found their mushrooms. You may ask about elevation to get a clue, and maybe you can inquire about what sort of habitat, but the exact spot? Nope, you've got to put in the work! Many mushroom species fruit in the same spot year after year, so finding a good patch of chanterelles, for example, is a very valuable piece of information. This can feel quite daunting to someone just starting out, but I like to think of it as an invitation to dig deeper. Many fungi have a symbiotic relationship with different tree and plant species. Get to know the trees that have a relationship with the mushrooms and you're more likely to find the mushrooms you're after. When you do find the mushrooms, take some time to pay attention. Notice everything that is happening around you. What's in bloom? What plants are nearby? How damp is the soil? What birds are singing? These are all clues that can help lead you to more mushrooms (and it's just a great life practice). Stop and smell the trees.

It's been a goal of mine for years to add a few new-to-me species each year. The world of mycology is so vast and overwhelming, and the number of days I can get out into the woods is nowhere near as many as I want it to be. So I don't overwhelm myself with a goal like being able to locate and identify every species, but instead aim to really get to know a few and then seek those out. Each year I add more, and now I've become confident with many species. When I'm diligent about taking notes and lots of photos in the field, that act also helps boost my mycological knowledge. It's a great activity in the winter, when many of the mushrooms are slumbering, to spend time looking over the notes and pictures from my years' forages and forays to try to identify the ones I found that I didn't know when I was looking at them in the woods.

Remember that we are just one part of the ecosystem and mushrooms are for more than just us. Take only what you need and can use when you get home. Of course, it's fun to share and I'm sure your friends and neighbors appreciate that. Many mushrooms do grow abundantly, and just like picking apples off the tree, picking mushrooms is not harmful to the fungus. But in the spirit of living in community, be aware of the delight other foragers may find upon stumbling on a patch and that other animals and insects use mushrooms for their sustenance as well. The mushrooms are not ours to hoard but rather to enjoy along with the rest of the natural world.

Leave the forest as you found it, or maybe even better than how you found it. By that I mean don't leave garbage, and consider adding a garbage bag to your mushroom kit to clean up someone else's trash. As a mom of three teenage kids, I'm already tired of cleaning up others' garbage, but in caring for our Earth, it's a small thing we can do to support our ecosystems.

Speaking of foraging kits, I generally bring a woven basket that allows for spores and other nature debris to fall back to the forest as I wander and gives the mushrooms loads of space, so they don't crush each other. I also carry a mushroom knife with a brush, a small field guide, plenty of water, a compass, a logbook, and a camera. For a foray you may want to include a small magnifying glass. I'll often bring along a tree identification guide as well whenever I'm out looking for mushrooms.

Field Notes from the Forest Floor

In the following section, we take a closer look at nearly fifty different species that share our Pacific Northwest home. From the delectably flavorful porcini (*Boletus edulis*, pages 38–41), boasting a brioche bun–like cap and a fragrance evocative of an Italian grandmother's kitchen, to the porous underbelly of the artist's conk (*Ganoderma applanatum*, page 66), serving as a covert canvas awaiting the artistic touch of a forest explorer.

We'll see mushrooms that "bleed" and others that "smoke." We'll explore the myths and lore that surround certain well known species, and we'll marvel at how the fungi connect us to the trees, plants, and other animals we share the Earth with. I'll point out which mushrooms are great for dyeing and which ones to avoid so there won't be any dying.

Join me as I share tales from my foraging escapades and impart some of my favorite insights and advice gained along the journey—some essential for navigating the woods, while others prove invaluable in the kitchen when bringing these mushrooms home.

Agaricus augustus

The prince

FAMILY: Agaricaceae

APPEARANCE: Large mushroom with warm brown tones and darker brown scales scattered all over the cap. The stem is smooth with scales at the lower portion, under the frilly skirt left from a partial veil.

HABITAT: Grows alone or in groups in disturbed areas like parks and landscaping.

SEASON: Summer and early fall

AGARICUS AUGUSTUS, COMMONLY KNOWN AS the prince mushroom, is renowned for its delightful sweet almond fragrance. This distinct aroma sets it apart from many other mushroom species and contributes to its popularity among foragers. I find that the almond or almond extract scent tends to soften as the mushroom ages or when it is cooked or dried. To me, the smell of a dried prince mushroom is delightfully reminiscent of cream of mushroom soup, which ironically I didn't like as a child, but this distinct fungal, deeply rich scent still holds a bit of nostalgia for me. For this reason, I like to dry my prince mushrooms and use them to create a rich stock and base for the ultimate cream of mushroom soup in the winter.

Agaricus augustus is quite large, with a cap that has scales the color of toasted marshmallow. Both the cap and the stem turn yellow if bruised. This mushroom typically fruits in the summer in damp soil under cedar trees. They also like disturbed areas, and on summer strolls around the neighborhood I've often found these fragrant mushrooms in landscaping. If you start looking for the prince when fall mushrooms are growing in abundance, you're likely too late as this is a warmer-weather mushroom.

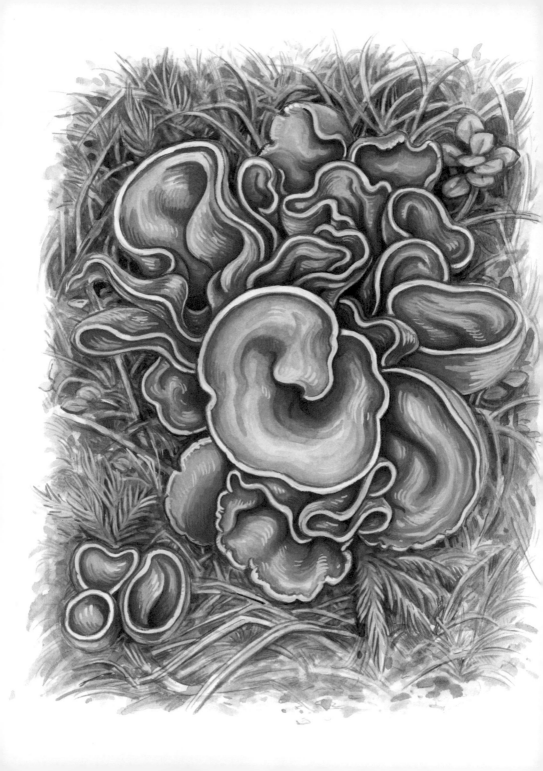

Aleuria aurantia

Orange peel fungus

FAMILY: Pyronemataceae

APPEARANCE: Bright orange cup shape. Slightly paler on the outside, almost looking dusty. More rounded when young, and edges start to furl as it ages.

HABITAT: Likes moist, disturbed soil.

SEASON: Fall (can also be seen in the spring)

IS THAT A DISCARDED ORANGE peel on the trail or the stunning *Aleuria aurantia*? I've been fooled before. It's always a delight to see this alluring (or should I say *aleur*-ing) mushroom in the woods as it stands in striking contrast to the decaying matter it likes to fruit in. The orange peel fungus is commonly found in disturbed areas with moist soil, such as grassy areas, lawns, meadows, and along forest roads and campsites. The spores of this mushroom evacuate when touched, and in the right light you may be able to see the spores disperse like a smoky cloud from the cup of this mushroom.

While *Aleuria aurantia* is technically edible, it is not commonly sought after for culinary purposes. It does, however, add color and protein to food. Some insist it can be eaten raw, while others say it must be cooked. Because of this inconsistent data I tend to leave this particular fungus to sporulate in the woods while I snap a quick photo or two before moving along and seeking out other, more delicious mushroom species.

Amanita muscaria

Fly agaric

FAMILY: Amanitaceae

APPEARANCE: Most notable by its bright red cap and white spots. Cap can also appear faded and orange. Narrow white gills just under the cap with a long stem and frilly ring. Scaly rings appear at the bulbous base where the universal veil was once attached.

HABITAT: Grows usually in small groupings in the soil with conifers like pine and spruce and some hardwoods.

SEASON: Fall

WHEN YOU HEAR OF MUSHROOMS, the image that likely pops into your mind is the *Amanita muscaria.* The imagery of this particular species can be seen in *Super Mario* video games, children's books including *Alice in Wonderland,* Disney's *Fanstasia,* and on all sorts of wildly popular mushroom merchandise.

Commonly known as fly agaric, this mushroom is believed to have been named after its use as a fly trap. When pieces of this mushroom were left soaking in milk, flies would be attracted by the scent, sip the mushroom milk, become intoxicated, and then drown in the liquid.

David Arora, mycologist and bestselling mushroom author, says that fly agarics are revered by both "maggots and mystics." Siberian shamans and Indigenous peoples in Scandinavia, including the Sami people, have been known to consume these mushrooms as entheogens, or psychoactive substances used to facilitate spiritual growth and development. Legend has it that these journeys are what served as inspiration for the figure of Santa Claus and his flying reindeer. Some continue the practice and swear by the healing properties of this psychoactive drug, but many reliable resources still warn of the potential toxicity and dangers of consumption.

This iconic fungus evokes diverse reactions, instilling profound fear in some, inducing intense spiritual experiences in others, and serving as a symbol that ignites myths, stories, and boundless wonders. Encountering this frequently spotted mushroom in its natural habitat still fills me with excitement. It proudly stands out amid the lush, moist forests of the Northwest, and I must confess, it captivates me.

Amanita phalloides

Death cap

FAMILY: Amanitaceae

APPEARANCE: Medium to large, classic stalk and cap shape when mature, begins as an oval shape. Cap is smooth and yellowish green. Death caps can have some color variance from olive green to brownish and white. If it hasn't rained in a bit, the cap will have a thin white patch. The gills are white to cream, and the spore print is white. There is a universal veil that covers the entire mushroom when young.

HABITAT: Grows alone or in small groupings in soil associated with hardwoods; often found around oak trees.

SEASON: Fall

AS A FUNGI LOVER, I consider it part of my mushroom mission to rid the world of fungi phobia, but this particular mushroom deserves every bit of its fearsome reputation. *Amanita phalloides,* the dreaded death cap mushroom, is known to be responsible for a staggering 90 percent of fungal fatalities. Its potency lies in the presence of amatoxins, causing severe liver and kidney damage, often leading to death. Astonishingly, just one cap holds enough toxins to be fatal for not just one but many individuals. What makes it even more treacherous is its deceptive appearance, often mimicking harmless mushrooms like the straw or paddy straw variety. This resemblance contributes to accidental poisonings, further exacerbated by the delayed onset of symptoms, typically occurring six to twenty-four hours after ingestion. The slowed connection between consumption and symptoms can delay vital medical attention. Unlike other toxic mushrooms, *Amanita phalloides* remain resistant to high temperatures or freezing, making cooking ineffective in neutralizing its toxins, unlike many other fearsome mushrooms. Interestingly, the death cap is believed to have arrived in North America through imported European trees. Awareness and caution are crucial when encountering this formidable fungus that defies appearances and holds a deadly secret. Although the death cap is a dangerous mushroom that should be avoided, it is still a precious part of our world that is interconnected in ways we have not begun to fully grasp.

Armillaria ostoyae

Dark honey fungus

FAMILY: Physalacriaceae

APPEARANCE: Cap
appears light to dark
brown with fibrous scales
when young. The gills are
creamy to white in color,
closely packed, and some-
what decurrent. The stem
is also white and cream in
color with light-brown or
gray patches. Partial veil
leaves a ring on the stem.

HABITAT: Fruits on
logs and softwoods like
Douglas fir and pine
trees. Can fruit on both
live and dead trees.

SEASON: Fall

ARMILLARIA OSTOYAE, OTHERWISE KNOWN AS the honey mushroom or dark honey fungus, gets that name not from its sweet temperament or flavor but rather from the color of the light-yellowish-brown cap with silky fibers that create a scaly texture around the cap when young. As the mushroom ages, the scales disappear and the cap appears smooth. The gills are tightly packed and white or cream in color, and the spore print is white. There is a ring present on the cream or tan stem. These mushrooms are, in fact, edible but require special preparation to make them safe to eat. Although some people have no issues when eating them, others experience stomach problems if they consume honey mushrooms without first boiling them for ten minutes. There have been no reported deaths or serious issues from eating this mushroom, but use caution when first trying it (or any mushroom). Taste and try a small bit the first time you eat it. The stems are tough and should be discarded before cooking. The flavor has been described as slightly sweet, earthy, fungal, and a little spicy with a chewy texture.

Far more interesting, in my opinion, than the fact that they can be eaten, is the huge reputation this mushroom has. You may have also heard the honey mushroom referred to as the destroyer of forests, tree killer, or Humongous Fungus. The mycelium of the particular species, named the largest living organism on Earth, is located in the Malheur National Forest in Eastern Oregon. This particular fungus is the size of nearly 1,800 football fields, covering 2,384 acres (3.7 square miles), and it's estimated to be between 2,000 and 8,000 years old, with some saying it could be even 9,600 years old. If you somehow managed to weigh the fungus in its entirety, it would weigh at least 7,500 tons, and possibly up to 35,000 tons, which is approximately the weight of about 250 gray whales.

The reason why scientists call this the largest living organism is because they have found this fungus with the exact same DNA reaching to the far corners of this forest. Let me explain: You see, it doesn't grow like other plants and animals. The growth of the *Armillaria ostoyae* happens through cloning. Reproducing sexually, the mushrooms (the fruiting bodies you see aboveground) release two different types of spores into the air. When one of each of the two types of spores finds the other, another fungus forms, one that is genetically identical to the original fungus, that is, a clone. This clone starts to grow and spread its mycelia. If the mycelia finds another genetically identical clone, they will fuse and become part of the same organism. After this process has repeated itself over thousands of years, you get the Humongous Fungus—what could possibly be the largest living organism on Earth.

I'll admit I find it more enjoyable to talk about the mushrooms that communicate with the trees, the ones that send resources back and forth in a reciprocal relationship, but that is not the case with *Armillaria ostoyae*. This fungus approaches a tree, then spreads rootlike rhizomorphs that creep their way under the bark and around the roots. They leach out the nutrients from the tree, killing the tree, a cartoonlike fungal villain dead set on destroying the planet—or just the trees. This process is quite slow, taking anywhere from twenty to fifty years to kill the trees. It's not *all* trees, however; they seem to have a preference for softwood trees like Douglas fir and pine. The reason why the Pacific Northwest has managed to be such a hospitable home to this enormous organism is because we have an abundance of these trees, providing a delectable feast for the honey fungus.

Armillaria ostoyae really aren't the villain, though, or perhaps better said, it's far more complex than good versus evil. The dead trees, or victims of the fungus, provide much-needed habitat for animals, and with the death of some of these tree varieties there's more opportunity for others to grow. Michael McWilliams, a pathologist with the US Forest Service, says it perfectly: "It's having a major ecological impact on this forest, and to me, anything that can do that is worth respecting." Like all things in nature and life, it's complicated.

Auricularia americana

Wood ear

FAMILY: Auriculariaceae

APPEARANCE: Ear-shaped or curving into a shallow bowl-like shape, typically brown or tan in color. The flesh is thin and rubbery and has a gelatinous texture.

HABITAT: Found on dead conifers, often in the same ecosystem where you would find morels.

SEASON: Commonly found year-round, particularly abundant in spring

INITIALLY RESEMBLING CUP-SHAPED STRUCTURES, THESE fungi develop lobes that bear a striking resemblance to human ears. On the outside, they show off a tan-brown and velvety appearance, while their inner surface appears shiny and wrinkled. The texture is gelatinous and quite rubbery. This mushroom has been used medicinally, particularly in Asian countries, for centuries. Medical studies have shown that wood ear mushrooms may help fight cancer, support heart health, are high in antioxidants, and can help protect against certain bacteria. *Auricularia americana* is indeed edible, although not many have given them much culinary credit in our part of the world. They are often sold dehydrated, then boiled until tender, three to five minutes, before being used in stir-fries or tossed with a soy sauce–based dressing and used in salads. If you happen upon *Auricularia americana* already dried and brittle in the wild, you can still harvest them and then rehydrate at home. In his book *Fruits of the Forest*, ethnomycologist Daniel Winkler writes of a mushroom farmer who rehydrates wood ears in a fragrant broth, then dehydrates them again for a crispy snack. I've often seen wood ear mushrooms when I'm out searching for *Morchella* sp. (pages 102–107), so while I don't often add this mushroom to my basket for taking home, I do get excited when I see them, as they often indicate that morels are likely nearby.

Boletus edulis

Porcini

FAMILY: Boletaceae

APPEARANCE: Lightly brown cap when young and shifts to reddish brown as it ages. Portly white stem covered in fine white netting called reticulation. Pores are white when young and turn yellow as they age. Firm flesh with a slight nutty scent.

HABITAT: You'll often find them alone or in groups growing along the edge of the forest with fir and spruce nearby. They love mountains and the constant, consistent moisture of coastal areas.

SEASON: Fall

BOLETUS EDULIS IS KNOWN BY many names: porcini, king bolete, king mushroom, penny bun, cep, giant cep. Whatever you want to call it, this mushroom is a prized edible and one of my absolute favorite mushrooms to find in the wild.

Boletus edulis has pores instead of gills; when young and still mostly under the ground, the pores will be white or creamy in color. As they age the pores turn yellow. The caps turn reddish brown as they age, but when young they look like a toasted hamburger bun. On the stem you'll notice some reticulation, which looks essentially as if the mushroom is wearing some white fishnet stockings. It's a fine webbing detail that adds an intricate pattern to the stem. While they can grow to an impressive size as they age, you'll want to look for them while they are still young and living mostly underground. So while hunting for porcini you're not necessarily looking for the mushroom, but what foragers call a *shrump*, which is a mounded, mini hill of soil and maybe some mosses, leaves, and needles, indicating that there is something lurking beneath the surface.

It is extremely rare, in my experience, to find a pristine porcini. Bugs adore this flavorful mushroom, which is another reason why it's best to find them young. However, I'm such a fan of this mushroom I tend to simply cut away the buggy parts and the elderly yellow parts. Dehydrating the porcini allows *most* of the bugs to fall away. If you'd rather not share your mushroom with them, you can use the porcini as a natural dye, with results ranging from tan to orange to yellow to olive green.

IN THE KITCHEN

It's where the king reigns.

One rain-free Halloween we decided to fire up the pizza oven to feed the crowd of kids before they went off trick-or-treating. Before dinner prep began, the adults went for a little walk. I wore my homemade papier-mâché *Amanita muscaria* hat and adjusted it ever so slightly just as I was about to point out to our friends where I had found a porcini a few weeks back. There, in the same spot, I noticed two more massive king bolete in a patch of grass just off the side of a quiet road in our neighborhood. Bugs and slugs had made a meal of most of one of these monstrous mushrooms, but we had enough that were bug-free to shave on our pizza and completely fill my dehydrator. The kids were more impressed with their candy haul from the evening, but I will never forget this treat from the earth.

To clean, use a sharp paring knife to cut away any parts that bugs have destroyed. If there are a few buggy holes, I leave those alone. Thinly shave away dirt or debris from the stem, and use a damp rag to wipe off any remaining twigs, pine needles, or other earthy bits.

My favorite way to eat porcini in their prime is thinly shaved on salads or pizzas, or with a bit of olive oil, lemon juice, and shaved Parmesan. Use a sharp mandoline to slice the mushrooms, then consume right away. They are also wonderful sautéed and dehydrate beautifully. It's my opinion that however you eat them, the porcini should be the star of the dish; they are the king after all.

Calvatia sculpta

Sculpted puffball

FAMILY: Agaricaceae

APPEARANCE: Rounded white mushroom with a sculpted top. Warts that cover the top extend to create pyramid-like shapes.

HABITAT: Mountainous areas usually associated with the ponderosa pine. East of the Cascades down into the Sierras.

SEASON: Spring/summer (April–August)

IMAGINE YOU'RE STROLLING ON A spring or summer hike, taking in the view of the conifer forests with the mountains as the backdrop. Suddenly, your gaze is caught by a sight that appears to be a piped meringue, delicately crafted by a pastry chef who has perhaps gotten a little carried away. Looking closer, you realize it's the *Calvatia sculpta,* known fondly as the sculpted puffball. The *Calvatia sculpta* is a member of the Agaricaceae family of fungi, and in addition to its stunning appearance, it is one of the more delectable puffballs. While young, when its flesh remains pristine white throughout, this marvelous mushroom may be sliced and woven into an array of culinary masterpieces, adding flavors akin to other savory mushrooms. Its dense nature allows it to effortlessly embrace a hot sizzling skillet, searing like a succulent steak. Once the interior starts to turn yellow, it's best to refrain from eating and simply marvel at this sculptural mushroom.

Beyond the kitchen, the puffball group in general boasts remarkable medicinal properties. Many Indigenous tribes across North America have used puffballs for treating wounds, their spores acting as natural antiseptics. In Chinese medicine, the spores of puffballs promote hemostasis and foster muscle regeneration. *Calvatia sculpta* isn't just a pretty sculpture hiding in the woods; it contains compounds that can both nourish and heal us.

Be aware that some *Amanita* varieties can look very similar to puffballs when young. As always, be sure you can identify your mushroom with 100 percent accuracy before ingesting.

Cantharellus formosus

Golden chanterelle

FAMILY: Cantharellaceae

APPEARANCE: Cap is golden orange, not quite as bright as an egg yolk, with a depressed center and wavy edges. They have false gills or ridges—folds that are often forking and run down the stem, gradually tapering off. The interior is bright white.

HABITAT: Always found growing on the ground, never on wood. Associates with Douglas fir, spruce, and pine. I've often found them on a mossy forest floor near salal.

SEASON: Late summer through fall

THE CHANTERELLE WILL ALWAYS HOLD a special place in my fungi-loving heart as it was the first species to lure me into the woods and kick-start my passion for foraging. Back in the days when I was only concerned with edible varieties, the chanterelle was also one of the first mushrooms that I enjoyed eating. They are one of the most widely known and recognized edible wild mushrooms. One of the best ways to identify a chanterelle is to open up the flesh to reveal its bright white interior. Daniel Winkler goes so far as to say, "It is downright depressing to imagine a mushroom-blessed existence without chanterelles!" I cannot think of chanterelles without hearing Daniel's voice shrieking, "A chanty!" as he did several times on a fall forage I did with him several years ago.

Chanterelles return year after year to the same spots and have mycorrhizal relationships with trees like Douglas fir, hemlock, pine, and spruce. That and the fact that they are brightly colored and easy to distinguish from other toxic look-alikes (see *Omphalotus olearius*, page 113) make them great for beginning foragers. The texture is very reminiscent of string cheese as it will pull apart easily in long, stringy pieces. When looking for these, just be prepared to have your hopes raised and then dashed by the similarly toned fallen leaves from nearby trees.

IN THE KITCHEN

I've used chanterelles in soups with late summer corn and a whisper of smoky bacon, in potpies bulked up with potatoes and cream and capped with a buttery crust, on toasts with creamy ricotta and drizzled with a spicy honey, and stirred into a simple pasta with loads of garlic and Parmesan. I've found chanterelles while camping and caramelized them (as you would an onion) with shallots and thyme, then topped a cast-iron pizza with them. They add an earthy, gentle umami flavor to pretty much any dish.

There's just one thing I'll urge you not to do with them: dry them. I've seen them dried; they are widely available that way. I suppose I'll allow it if you're just planning on turning them into a powder and using them as a mushroom seasoning, but there are better varieties for that (hello, morels). Rehydrated chanterelles are tough and never get their fresh texture back. To preserve them, it's better to freeze sautéed chanterelles into small portions to tuck into soups, stews, braises, and pasta dishes. You can also pickle them with fresh herbs, garlic, a bit of oil, loads of vinegar, and a touch of honey. These are lovely served in a salad, on a cheese plate, or to top a cheesy toast.

Cantharellus subalbidus

White chanterelle

FAMILY: Cantharellaceae

APPEARANCE: The cap is often depressed in the center and wavy around the edges. The white chanterelle is white or creamy in color with false gills that are actually ridges or folds that run partially down the stem.

HABITAT: Found on the ground in association with Douglas fir or western hemlock.

SEASON: Fall

I'M NOT SURE IF IT'S due to their white color or the way they seem to hide from me in the woods, but the white chanterelle evokes a ghostlike image in my mind. These mushrooms share a similar habitat to the matsutake and tend to prefer drier environments than the golden chanterelle. I'm told their flavor is similar to that of a golden chanterelle, but people insist that their texture is preferred.

There are several look-alikes that you need to be aware of, but if you are comfortable identifying golden chanterelles in the wild, it won't take much for you to familiarize yourself with this species. They can be confused with the short-stemmed brittlegill (*Russula brevipes,* page 132), but the white chanterelle turns yellow when handled or bruised and the brittlegill does not. Also, be aware of some white *Amanitas* that look similar. These *Amanita* varieties do have true gills, so be sure you are looking for the folds on your white chanterelles.

Chlorociboria aeruginascens

Blue-stain fungus

FAMILY: Chlorociboriaceae

APPEARANCE: You'll likely see the work of this fungus through its bluish-green-staining mycelium in the wood it decays.

HABITAT: It generally prefers shaded, moist environments and is commonly observed growing on logs, fallen branches, or decaying stumps on the forest floor, particularly on bark-free wood like oak.

SEASON: Winter to early spring

TEAL IS NOT A COLOR found frequently in the woods and yet, if you're paying attention, you may stumble upon a striking piece of blue-green wood. The bluish-green or teal color of the wood is the work of a fungus, *Chlorociboria aeruginascens*, commonly known as the blue-stain fungus or green elfcup. Even more rare than spotting blue wood in the forest is being able to find the turquoise-colored fruiting body of this fungus. If you were to find it, you would see a cup fungus in a striking teal color usually no larger than 1 to 3 cm. The mycelium of the fungus breaking down the decaying wood is what gives the wood its eye-catching color and the common name green oak. Green oak has been used by artists and woodworkers for centuries to create decorative inlaid pieces. Sharing in my delight of a wood-painting fungus, Isabel Hardman, author of *The Natural Health Service*, says, "The surprise we feel on seeing the Green Elfcup teaches us that the most limited thing is not nature, but our own imaginations."

Coprinus comatus

Shaggy mane

FAMILY: Agaricaceae

APPEARANCE: When young, the cap is conical and egg-shaped, looking like a rounded column. As it matures, the cap becomes bell-shaped. Light brown on top with feathery scales. Smooth, slender stem that is hollow with a wide, bulbous base. The gills are white and tightly packed when young but quickly turn black as the shaggy mane ages.

HABITAT: Grassy, disturbed areas such as golf courses, parks, fields, lawns, meadows, driveways, and roadsides.

SEASON: Summer through fall

COPRINUS COMATUS, COMMONLY KNOWN AS either shaggy mane or shaggy ink cap mushroom, has a distinctive appearance, which makes it great for beginning foragers. In addition to being easy to spot, it also grows widely in places where people are. When young, the fruiting body looks like a hairy egg or, to me, a classic cartoon-ghost shape on a thin stipe. The cap is white and ovoid, covered in shaggy white or grayish-brown scales.

Here's the wild part: In the span of less than twenty-four hours, *Coprinus comatus* undergoes an autodigestion process called deliquescing. While maturing, the mushroom experiences rapid autolysis, or the destruction of tissues or cells by their own enzymes, causing the gills and cap to dissolve into an inky black liquid. You may be wondering, "Why does this mushroom start digesting itself and turn into a gooey black pool?" It's because of spore dispersal. The gills of the shaggy mane are packed so closely together that spores are unable to do what spores are meant to do—disperse. This problem is solved by turning the mushroom into liquid; the edges of the unfurled cap begin to curl, exposing the opened gills to the air, allowing the spores to disperse through the air currents as the liquid drops and releases spores back into the soil.

Coprinus comatus is considered a choice edible and is a favorite among many foragers. However, it is important to note that this mushroom should only be eaten when young, before the cap starts to autodigest and turn into ink. Shaggy mane mushrooms are commonly found growing together, so if you find one, you're likely to find several more nearby. Finding these mushrooms when young and in prime shape for eating is rare as they are usually already in the process of decay. I have often found them on the side of the road while driving, or while on a walk, and by the time I got home they were already black and inky. For this reason, the most common way I like to enjoy *Coprinus comatus,* besides just marveling at their little white ghostlike appearance in the wild, is to make ink.

MAKING INK WITH *COPRINUS COMATUS*

Collect the mushrooms, then store in a lidded jar in the fridge and wait for them to break down, three to four days. Once broken down, you should be left with an inky liquid. Strain the ink into a jar, or you can leave the mushroom pieces to provide some interesting texture to your art. Add some salt, whole cloves, or a few drops of thyme, tea tree, lavender, or mint essential oils as a preservative for the ink. If you want to concentrate the ink for a deeper color, you could simmer and reduce until slightly thickened. (The illustration on page 55 was made using this ink!)

Craterellus calicornucopioides

Black trumpet

FAMILY: Cantharellaceae

APPEARANCE: Black or dark brown funnel-shaped mushroom. Stem is hollow and lighter in color than the top of the mushroom.

HABITAT: Grows on the ground or on nearly fully decayed wood, particularly around white oak.

SEASON: Late fall into early winter

CRATERELLUS CALICORNUCOPIOIDES IS HIGHLY celebrated among mushroom enthusiasts due to its rich, smoky, and earthy taste. Resembling an inverted trumpet, the black trumpet mushroom has a distinctive appearance with deep ridges, occasional wrinkles, and edges that elegantly roll back. There's a catch, though—because it's darkly colored and likes to hide out amid leaf litter and rich, loamy soil, the black trumpet is often hard to spot. This mushroom is particularly suitable for dehydration as this process intensifies the flavors. Additionally, it possesses a sturdy structure that allows for thorough washing—a desirable attribute as its cone-shaped form tends to accumulate pine needles, small twigs, and insects. Look for these mushrooms in areas with diverse hardwood trees such as oaks, beech, and maple. Seek out washes—swampy or marshy regions located on hill slopes or depressions. While they are not typically found in mud or water, they are often near such environments. These mushrooms may appear individually or in clusters.

They are sometimes referred to as the poor man's truffle—they won't fetch the same price as a truffle, but their flavor is one to seek out. I must admit that the only time I've found these mushrooms is at my local farmers' market, where my favorite commercial foragers were selling them. Until I find them in the woods myself, I will continue to stock up in early winter, when I generously bathe them in a cheesy cream sauce with roasted cauliflower and a crisp breadcrumb and Parmesan crust.

Craterellus tubaeformis

Winter chanterelle

FAMILY: Cantharellaceae

APPEARANCE: The cap is typically dark brown to blackish and deeply wrinkled, while the tubelike structures are a bright yellow color. On the underside are wrinkles that look like gills but aren't uniform, similar to chanterelles.

HABITAT: Fruiting on decaying conifer wood and in moist soil and moss.

SEASON: Fall through winter

CRATERELLUS TUBAEFORMIS, ALSO KNOWN AS winter chanterelle or yellowfoot, is a small to medium-sized mushroom with a funnel-shaped cap and a hollow, tubelike stem. It typically grows in clusters on the forest floor, particularly in coniferous and mixed woodlands. It is often ignored by foragers in search of the more well-known varieties such as the chanterelle. Yellow feet, referring to the bright yellow stem, are similar in flavor to the chanterelle, and while they are quite a bit smaller, they often grow in abundance so you can quickly fill a small basket if you happen upon them.

They are great sautéed with butter or oil and a little shallot or garlic. They also dry nicely and can be rehydrated by pouring just boiled water over the top. When foraging, take care not to crush this fragile mushroom. I recommend keeping them away from other varieties in your basket as they easily fall apart.

Dacrymyces chrysospermus

Witch's butter

FAMILY:
Dacrymycetaceae

APPEARANCE: Bright yellow-orange fruiting body with a jelly-like texture. Frilly folds wrinkle together to resemble a small brain-like structure. Attaching to the wood it grows on with a tough white base.

HABITAT: Fruits on dead conifers are often found in groupings.

SEASON: Commonly found in late fall and early winter

THE COMMON NAME WITCH'S BUTTER can be a bit tricky since it refers to several different species, and pinpointing the exact one can be a challenge. In order to know exactly which species, you need to pay attention to the trees. This is a common invitation from the mushrooms that I appreciate. It's almost as if they're telling us, "Stop and smell the conifers." That's precisely where you'll find the species known as *Dacrymyces chrysospermus*—well, specifically on deceased conifers.

This particular type of witch's butter is edible but bland. What it lacks in color, it makes up for in a pop of bright yellow-orange color that adds visual excitement to a dish. While foraging with a friend, I found a few witch's butter mushrooms growing on a nearby log. With baskets full of a variety of fungi, we cooked a feast of mushrooms over the campfire. Our witch's butter added a delicate flavor and a lovely orange glow to our salad, which we also topped with more sautéed mushrooms.

Fistulina hepatica

Beefsteak polypore

FAMILY: Fistulinaceae

APPEARANCE: The surface of the cap ranges in color from pinkish beige to deep red depending on age. The pores are white or creamy in color.

HABITAT: Grows alone or in small groupings on the lower trunks of oaks, sweet chestnuts, and other members of the beech family.

SEASON: Fall and early winter

FISTULINA HEPATICA GETS ITS COMMON names, beefsteak or ox-tongue fungus, from its striking appearance, which bears an uncanny resemblance to a slab of raw meat, even going so far as to "bleed" when you cut into it. It has a streaked or marble flesh, taking its job of imitating meat quite seriously. Unfortunately, the flavor is found quite lacking by many. Some report it has quite a sour taste, which could be mitigated by parboiling, or you can lean into the sour lemonlike flavor and serve it as a sort of carpaccio. When found young, thinly slice the beefsteak onto a serving platter, sprinkle with shaved Parmesan or pecorino, drizzle with a fruity and grassy olive oil, add a pinch of flake salt, and finish with a bit of Italian parsley. Don't get too excited, though, as this is quite a rare find in the Northwest since it loves oak trees and young chestnuts, which are not abundant in the area.

Fomitopsis mounceae

Western red-belted conk

FAMILY: Fomitopsidaceae

APPEARANCE: Begins as a white or pale-yellow knob growing off dead trees in the pine family. As it ages, the top becomes reddish brown with a reddish or red-orange band at the rim. The underside remains white or creamy yellow as it ages, with tiny pores.

HABITAT: Grows as a shelflike structure alone or in groups on dead trees, logs, and stumps. Commonly found on pines, firs, hemlocks, and spruce.

SEASON: Year-round

FOMITOPSIS MOUNCEAE IS ONE OF the most abundant and common conks found in the Northwest. This prolific tree recycler plays a crucial role in breaking down dead trees, transforming them into nutrient-dense soil that sustains a vibrant ecosystem. *Fomitopsis mounceae* is named after Canadian mycologist, Irene Mounce. You'll likely find their distinctive "shelves" on fallen trees and stumps in the pine family, including firs, pines, hemlock, and spruce. Its reddish caps feature an outer orange or red-orange rim, earning it the common name, Western red-belted conk. It was also known as tinderwood fungus since Native tribes, including the Blackfoot in Alberta, and early settlers used it as a reliable fire starter because the dense interior stays dry, a rare occurrence in our damp climate. Additionally, its dried and ground form was used as a wound treatment, with the powder packed into injuries to stop any bleeding. It's also an immunomodulating mushroom, which means that it contains a substance that adjusts the immune system to make it work more effectively. It may help the body fight cancer, infection, or other diseases. Western red-belted conk can be finely ground and added to stocks and broths to infuse the stock with some of those immune-boosting compounds.

Ganoderma applanatum

Artist's conk

FAMILY: Ganodermataceae

APPEARANCE: Grows shelflike in an irregular fan shape with grays, browns, and sometimes black covering the cap. The underside is white when fresh but bruises brown.

HABITAT: Grows alone or in groups on hardwood logs and stumps, or can be found growing out of wounds on live trees.

SEASON: Year-round

RESTING UPON MY MANTEL, A dried *Ganoderma applanatum* takes pride of place. Years ago, my niece's nimble hand etched an intricate salmon onto the fungus's porous white canvas, proving its use as the artist's conk. This tough, long-lasting shelf fungus can live for many years. Growth ridges on the top surface and layers of pores inside, like tree rings, can tell you its age. Releasing spores by the billions, *Ganoderma applanatum* will cover its surrounding area with a dense brown dust, which almost looks as if someone has sifted the area with cocoa powder. Similar to *Fomitopsis mounceae*, *Ganoderma applanatum* is a medicinal fungus revered in Asian cultures for its immune-boosting, anti-inflammatory, and anti-tumor properties. It also plays a crucial role in supporting forest ecosystems as a decomposer, breaking down wood and recycling nutrients. The dried masterpiece adorning my mantel could just as well find a home in an art gallery as a medicine cabinet.

Ganoderma oregonense

Reishi

FAMILY: Ganodermataceae

APPEARANCE: A poly-pore that grows shelflike on wood. Medium to large shiny cap (although it could look powdery from spores of nearby reishi), ranging in color from reddish brown to orange and white. The pore surface underneath is creamy in color and browns easily if disturbed or when it's dried.

HABITAT: Commonly found growing on conifers in aging forests.

SEASON: Summer through fall

ON THE DAY I FOUND my first reishi in the wild, I already knew of its medicinal properties. I was aware that reishi has been used in traditional Chinese medicine for centuries and is commonly known as the mushroom of immortality. I had heard of its ability to help regulate the immune system, its calming effects, and its amazing antiviral capabilities. So when I spotted the glistening brown cap of the reishi on a fallen hemlock tree while hiking, I absolutely fangirled.

In recent groundbreaking studies led by Paul Stamets and Washington State University, wood-rotting fungi that are a rich source of antiviral compounds have been used to help save bee populations. The introduction of a 1 percent extract derived from amadou (*Fomes*) and reishi (*Ganoderma*) into the sugar water of bees led to an eightyfold decrease in deformed wing virus. The science (as of this writing) is still very young, but one of the keys to its success is getting the word out so that more research can be done and these medicines can be widely used. In this interconnected mycelium web we all live in, each of us is being asked to play a role. To get the medicinal benefits from this mushroom, you can dry pieces of it and use it in a tea, dry and grind into a powder, or make a tincture.

There are other species of reishi, but what we commonly find in our woods here in the Pacific Northwest, typically growing on dead hemlock, is the species known as *Ganoderma oregonense,* or Oregon reishi.

Geastrum saccatum

Earthstar

FAMILY: Geastraceae

APPEARANCE: Round and bulblike when young. As it ages, the outer wall splits and rays unfold like petals. Eventually they bend back under the spore case. The spore case is round, smooth, and usually a dull gray-brown.

HABITAT: Growing solitary or in small groups in the dirt under trees. They can usually exist for a few weeks or months without decay.

SEASON: Fall and winter

THE *GEASTRUM SACCATUM*, OR EARTHSTAR, looks to me like a cartoon drawing of a flower. It is one of the few earthstar varieties well suited to the region's moist conifer forests, despite the general preference of many other earthstars for drier ecosystems. The spore case, which is central to the fruiting body, is surrounded by four to eight rays that appear like rubbery petals. In the center of the spore case is a small pore that when disturbed, either by rain, animal, or curious forager, emits a puff of brown powder that looks a bit like smoke but is actually millions of spores dispersing.

The release of spores in this manner turned early taxonomists into toilet-humor-loving ten-year-olds: *Lycoperdon,* which is another genus of puffball mushrooms, literally means "wolf fart," and *Bovista,* commonly known as true puffballs, means "ox fart." This particular group of spore-releasing wonders belongs to the genus *Geastrum,* a delightful combination of *geo,* meaning "earth," and *astrum,* meaning "star"—a nod to both the playful and poetic world of nature. I must admit, the thought of those early taxonomists huddled together, chuckling like schoolkids about farts and mushrooms, brings a smile to my face too. This just goes to show that even in the world of science, a good sense of humor and a sense of awe go hand in hand.

Gomphus clavatus

Pig's ear

FAMILY: Gomphaceae

APPEARANCE:
Distinctive cup or
wedgelike shape with a
light-purple exterior and
tan or light-brown on the
top of the cap. Wrinkly
ridgelike veins cover
the exterior much like a
chanterelle. The flesh is
white, firm, and stringy
when pulled apart.

HABITAT: Typically grows
in clusters in rotted wood
in conifer forests.

SEASON: Late summer
through fall

OCCASIONALLY REFERRED TO AS THE purple chanterelle
due to its exterior ridges resembling those of the chanterelle mushroom, the pig's ear displays a delightful, gentle
lilac hue. *Gomphus clavatus* (a Latin name quite enjoyable to pronounce) is considered a choice edible option
among foragers. When young, the flesh has a firm texture,
but as the mushroom ages, the purple color deepens and
it becomes mealy and astringent. You may have to com-
pete with the bugs for this mushroom as they also find
this variety enjoyable and often beat us human foragers to
it. *Gomphus clavatus* often grow in abundant groupings,
so if you see a few, you'll likely encounter more nearby.
But there are also reports of a rapid decline in this species
as they are losing more and more of their habitat. Here
in the Northwest, they tend to like old-growth forests,
specifically preferring conifers. I've yet to find and cook
with these mushrooms, but I've heard that the texture is
similar to a lobster mushroom (pages 83–85)—firm and
even a bit crunchy, with a flavor that is rich and meaty.
They are well suited as a meat substitute in a taco with
roasted corn and a smoky salsa, or they can withstand
long braises.

Gyromitra esculenta

False morel

FAMILY: Discinaceae

APPEARANCE: Brain-like folds, wrinkled surface with a cap that is lobed and irregularly shaped. Cap color ranges from red-brown to muted red with a stipe that can be light tan or sometimes reddish brown like the cap.

HABITAT: Damp soil around hardwoods and conifers. Can be found on decaying wood.

SEASON: Spring/early summer (in cooler climates)

GYROMITRA ESCULENTA IS OFTEN REFERRED to as brain mushroom, false morel, beefsteak morel, or elephant's ear. These names reflect its distinctive appearance, which includes a brain-like, convoluted cap and an irregular shape with colors that range from pale yellow to reddish brown. *Esculenta* is derived from a Latin word that means "edible" or "food," and while historically it has been eaten, it's important to note that *Gyromitra esculenta* contains a toxic compound called gyromitrin. Extended boiling or soaking in water is essential to remove toxins before consumption. For this reason, and the fact that there are many other mushrooms to enjoy on your dinner plate, I like to just appreciate this one while in the field. There have been reported cases of poisonings, but many of them are due to the fact that this mushroom tends to get confused with the morel.

Similar to natural morels, this mushroom prefers damp areas with organic matter, such as moss-covered forest floors. It emerges near hardwood trees and conifers, stumps, or fallen logs during spring and early summer, so if you see *Gyromitra esculenta*, the morels are likely nearby. To distinguish it from morels, note the stems of *Gyromitra esculenta* are not hollow, unlike the fused stems and caps of morels, which form a single cavity (see pages 102–107).

Hericium abietis

Bear's head

FAMILY: Hericiaceae

APPEARANCE: *Hericium abietis* comes in a variety of sizes and can often grow to be quite large, with colors that range from white to delicate pale pink. The dangling teethlike structures can be up to 1 cm long. It grows clustered and in a branching form.

HABITAT: Dead conifers, especially fir and Douglas fir. Appears year after year on the same logs.

SEASON: Summer to late fall

ON A SOMEWHAT DISAPPOINTING MUSHROOM foray, a couple of friends and I were walking back toward the car with nearly empty baskets. They were up ahead a little ways while I stayed behind, marveling at the beauty of the old growth on an atypically warm fall afternoon. Out of the corner of my eye I spotted a large patch of white. It was well off the trail and required a bit of climbing over fallen trees, but when I reached the site of this mushroom, it was all worth it. Nearly seven pounds of a pristine *Hericium abietis*, or bear's head mushroom.

This shaggy white fruiting body resembles a bear's noble head or a lion's flowing mane, adorned with long, dangling spines instead of typical mushroom caps. (Unlike typical mushrooms with pores or gills, the bear's head mushroom has teeth from which its spores are released.) This extraordinary fungus befriends coniferous trees, particularly firs, spruces, and pines, growing elegantly on their trunks and branches. The culinary world reveres the bear's head for its unique taste and texture. With a mild, slightly sweet flavor and a firm, seafood-like texture, it becomes a favorite in vegetarian and vegan dishes. Langdon Cook, the esteemed forager and writer, who was with me when we found this mushroom, encouraged me to make "crab" cakes as the mushroom's texture and flavor are quite similar to the crustacean's. Back home in the kitchen, I sliced up about one and half pounds of the mushroom and sautéed it in a bit of oil. From there, I mixed it with all the ingredients used in my favorite crab cake recipe, replacing the crab with the sautéed bear's head. The flavor was very similar to the crab cakes I'm used to, although the lemon flavor was more pronounced as the mushrooms absorbed more flavor than crab typically does. We could only eat so many cakes, so the rest of the mushroom went into the dehydrator to become the base of many stocks and mushroom powders.

Research hints at the bear's head's potential medicinal properties, such as boosting immunity and stimulating neurons to regrow.

Hydnellum peckii

Bleeding tooth

FAMILY: Bankeraceae

APPEARANCE: When young, this mushroom appears as dense whitish lumps with red liquid oozing from the cap. They change from beige to brown to black as they mature.

HABITAT: Prefers mature, species-rich forest with rich soil covered in organic material. Found near Douglas fir, fir, hemlock, spruce, and pine.

SEASON: Late summer to early fall

HYDNELLUM PECKII, OTHERWISE KNOWN AS bleeding tooth fungus or devil's tooth, is a unique mushroom that is neither toxic nor delicious, but what it lacks in flavor and fear factor it makes up for in absolute oddity. When young, the white mushroom appears to be bleeding, as stark red liquid oozes from the cap. When the earth is thoroughly drenched, water from the forest floor is pulled into the mushroom through osmosis. Because of a pigment found within the mushroom, the rainwater is transformed into a ruby-colored liquid, turning this mushroom into one of the most striking and unique fungi around. *Hydnellum peckii* is mycorrhizal and often associated with Douglas fir, fir, hemlock, spruce, and pine. They prefer the lush soil of mature forests carpeted with organic material such as fallen leaves. You'll often find them in the same forests where chanterelles, lobster mushrooms, and hedgehogs lurk.

The bleeding tooth fungus possesses medicinal properties, although the exact nature of the red substance it oozes remains unknown. However, scientists have discovered that it contains a pigment with anticoagulant and antibacterial properties. Additionally, there is another substance within it that shows potential for treating Alzheimer's disease. *Hydnellum peckii* is also highly valued by natural dyers, who dry it and then use it to create a beige dye or combine it with mordants, such as alum or iron, to produce blue-green hues. As the mushroom ages, it transitions from red to brown and eventually black when fully mature. You'll only see this mushroom "bleed" when young.

Hypomyces lactifluorum

Lobster mushroom

FAMILY: Hypocreaceae

APPEARANCE: Bright orange and red in color. The surface is smooth when young, then develops small bumps and a rough texture. You'll likely see non-parasitized short-stemmed brittlegills (*Russula brevipes,* page 132) growing nearby.

HABITAT: Usually growing in small groups with most of the fruiting body still covered by the duff in conifer forests.

SEASON: Late summer into fall

HERE, THE STORY TAKES A dark turn as we witness a form of fungus-on-fungus cannibalism. The lobster mushroom isn't actually a mushroom, but the result of a fungal attack on the short-stemmed brittlegill. When the *Hypomyces lactifluorum* fungus infects these mushrooms, it transforms their appearance, giving them a vibrant red or orange color that resembles cooked lobster, or as I like to describe it, the color of Cheetos. It grows on and consumes the host mushroom, eventually replacing it entirely. This unique transformation and the slightly seafood-tinged scent has earned it the common name lobster mushroom.

Because of the bright color and easy-to-distinguish features, this a great mushroom for beginners to identify. It's also perfect for getting kids out into the woods because they love the idea of one fungus eating another and the bright orange, seemingly unnatural color makes it easy to spot. You may have to root around in the dirt, though, as they first appear hidden under the duff and you may notice only a small bit of orange. After some quick digging, you'll often uncover a fairly large mushroom. Adding to its intrigue, the lobster mushroom stands as one of the season openers of the fall fruiting months because of its ability to survive in dry conditions and its resistance to rotting. They seem to like environments where I often also find chanterelles. There's likely moss on the ground, salal growing in abundance, and coniferous trees growing all around.

IN THE KITCHEN

The parasitic process of this fungi changes its host into a fragrant and flavorful mushroom that I find irresistible. It dehydrates beautifully and can be turned into an aromatic mushroom powder that packs a soft punch of flavors of the sea. It adds a bright pop of color to pastas and risottos, and a fungal umami to braises and stews. The texture is quite sturdy; it can withstand long braises and simmering dishes quite well. Not long ago, my friend encountered a cluster of lobsters and prepared a successful tikka masala using the mushrooms in place of chicken. I've also heard that they are prepared as a meat substitute in Mexico, where they are first boiled, then sautéed with tomatoes and onions and eaten with tortillas.

Be aware that there are some who have experienced gastrointestinal distress after consuming the lobster. Eat only a small amount the first time to see how well you tolerate this species. If you're one of the few who finds consuming these fungi a bit bothersome, you can instead turn to the dyer's pot. The lobster mushroom, when mixed with various mordants (substances used to set the dye to the fibers or fabric), can produce a powerful dye in a range of colors from peach, pink, orange, and red to purple and blue.

Lactarius rubidus

Candy cap

FAMILY: Russulaceae

APPEARANCE: Small
mushroom with decurrent
gills that run down the
stem; rusty brown or burnt
orange in color.

HABITAT: Along trails or
wet soil in Douglas fir or
hemlock forests, especially
abundant around decaying
wood and leaf litter, particularly alder leaves.

SEASON: Late fall

WITH ITS VIBRANT RUSTY BROWN or burnt-orange cap, *Lactarius rubidus* is a true standout in the fungal kingdom. When dried or cooked, this mushroom undergoes a chemical transformation and emits an enticing aroma reminiscent of maple syrup or butterscotch, earning its delightful nickname, candy cap. Chefs and daring cooks with a sweet tooth eagerly seek it out to infuse their dishes with a distinct maplelike taste, whether it's desserts, ice creams, or even savory creations like soups and sauces. Most often, those looking to add sweetness from candy caps will dry, then grind the mushrooms to create a fine, sweet powder. This powder can be used in baked goods, infused into creams, or sprinkled on top of a sweet or savory dish for an added boost of a toasted, sugary flavor. However, because the sweet aroma is only present once the mushroom is heated or dried, this desirable characteristic won't serve as a distinguishing factor in the woods. To confirm its presence, mushroom guide and author Daniel Winkler suggests bringing a lighter into the woods to detect the fragrance when heated.

Laetiporus conifericola

Chicken of the woods

FAMILY: Fomitopsidaceae

APPEARANCE: Large fruiting body that often appears like a candy corn, ranging in colors of various yellows and orange. Fruits in a fan shape with a smooth suede-like surface. The underside has pale yellow pores.

HABITAT: Grows in shelving clusters on mature conifers. Usually found on dead trees, but has been found on trees that are still alive.

SEASON: After late-summer rain and into the fall

LAETIPORUS CONIFERICOLA, OTHERWISE KNOWN AS chicken of the woods, is one mushroom that makes itself known in the forest, as if it is inviting you to find it. Its brilliant yellow and orange colors stand in striking contrast against the conifer trees it grows on. *Laetiporus conifericola* is one of a few great edible polypores we can find growing in the Northwest. Polypores are a group of fungi that produce large fruiting bodies with pores or tubes on the underside. Many have a long history of medicinal uses but most are deemed inedible because of their tough, wood-like texture. Here in the Northwest we have a couple of delicious polypores including cauliflower mushroom (page 135). Chicken of the woods grows in shelflike clusters, indicating its other common name, sulphur shelf, and can often be found growing in great abundance on just one tree. If you find this fungi and it's past its prime, mark the location and then come back earlier next year, after a good summer rain. Chicken of the woods return year after year in the same spot if the conditions are right. This mushroom is full of water, lending to its tender texture when young, and can be quite heavy.

IN THE KITCHEN

Refrain from eating if the chicken of the woods shows signs of age and decay. The best time to eat this mushroom is when it is very young, when the flesh is firm but pliable and when you notice a wet, almost creamy-looking liquid that oozes once cut. Avoid eating if you notice any discoloration; it should be various shades of bright orange and yellow. Remove any bits of the mushrooms that are browning or dark as this is caused by bacteria that has been shown to be toxic, according to mycologist Paul Stamets, and gives the mushroom a sour taste. This mushroom must be cooked thoroughly before ingesting. When the chicken of the woods is raw or undercooked, some people have reported allergic reactions. When young, it is safe and delicious to eat the entire fruiting body. As the mushroom ages, you'll want to cook the fresh edge. Timing is key when finding this mushroom since the older mushrooms develop a tough texture that's more akin to cardboard than tender chicken. In fact, it is the texture of this mushroom that gives it its common name. It is similar to chicken and can be prepared in a similar way. If the mushroom feels tough, it will be tough! So find it young and only use the parts that are tender.

Prepare as you would chicken. I've seen many people marinate strips of tender chicken of the woods in buttermilk, then batter and fry to make "chicken" strips. While foraging in Alaska, our guide prepared a barbecue "chicken" pizza with our finds from the day. On a recent camping trip, we found a fresh patch of chicken of the woods on a hike, then returned to the campsite to make "chicken" tacos for dinner.

Slices of tender chicken of the woods can also be dehydrated, then turned into a flavorful powder to use in seasoning salts, marinades, soups, and stocks. You can dehydrate sautéed or fresh chicken of the woods, but if you dehydrate them fresh you'll still need to cook the mushroom before ingesting. So use the mushroom powder only in a finishing salt that will have heat applied to it. It is best to cook the mushrooms before freezing.

Lepista nuda

Wood blewit

FAMILY: Tricholomataceae

APPEARANCE: Lilac-colored cap and gills when young. As the mushroom ages, the cap fades to a very light purple and then eventually to a light brown. The stem is also light purple and looks faintly scaly or fibrous.

HABITAT: Fruits in leaf litter and other organic debris. Can be found in gardens and compost.

SEASON: Fall into early winter

ONE OF THE DISTINGUISHING ELEMENTS of this mushroom is the color. When young, the wood blewit is a striking lilac color that stands out in the leaf litter where it likes to grow. As it ages, the color fades to light purple, then tan and light brown.

Another way this mushroom stands out is its scent, which is often described as citrusy, like orange juice or even orange juice concentrate. Some say it's a mix of citrus and perfume. The aroma, although not detectable by everyone, distinguishes the wood blewit from other poisonous look-alikes like the pale blewit, grass blewit, or violet webcaps. If you've not picked up on the scent, you can do a spore print. To do a spore print, remove the cap from the stem and place on a piece of paper or glass, cover the cap with a cup or small bowl, then leave undisturbed for twelve to twenty-four hours. Wood blewits release spores that are softly pink. *Lepista nuda* is edible but should never be consumed raw.

Leucangium carthusianum

Oregon black truffle

FAMILY: Morchellaceae

APPEARANCE: Round and knobby. The black truffle is black on the outside, resembling a bit of coal. Usually they are about the size of a walnut but have been found bigger. The inside is solid with marbling of white and dark brown.

HABITAT: Found with Douglas firs west of the Cascades.

SEASON: Fall through spring, depending on the species

TRUFFLES FRUIT UNDERGROUND, WHICH PROTECTS the fruiting body from extreme temperatures, making them a favorite to forage in the winter. Despite hiding underground, they make use of their fragrance to lure woodland creatures who help the fungi by eating the fruiting body, then dispersing the spores hopefully near some of the mycorrhizal plants and Douglas fir trees they associate with. Because of this, they are generally found with the help of a trained dog. Some determined foragers have been known to use rakes, but the aggressive digging can be quite damaging to the ecosystem.

Long before I became a fanatical fan of fungi, I fell in love with truffles. Like many food-love stories, it began in Italy: tableside-shaved truffles on top of hand-rolled noodles in a slick sauce of eggs and crystalline Parmesan. It was a scent and flavor I had never experienced, and I do not exaggerate when I tell you that tears formed in the corners of my eyes and a giant smile grew on my face. This event was the first of many bites that shifted my life path away from art educator to food professional, and as they say: the rest is history.

Years later, I still believed that it was only in Italy or France that I could live out my truffle dreams. Then I met Alana McGee, from the Truffle Dog Company, a spunky, passionate expert who blends her love of dogs and her love of fungi into an enviable career. She agreed to take my husband, brother, and me out into the woods. One extremely rainy day in January (even for Northwest standards), we went out to forage—though in the case of truffles, it's more of a "follow the incredibly trained dogs around on an underground goose chase". They pick up the scent, then take off into the woods. Once they are on top of the scent, they furiously start digging until they unearth the tuber. A young or novice dog may start to gnaw on the fragrant fungus before you reach them and can pry it away by dangling a piece of chicken.

Now, I will not pretend that our Northwest black truffles are the same as the ones more readily found in Italy and France, but when I found out that we have native truffles my love for the Northwest only grew stronger. The truffles we found on the day of our hunt were *Leucangium carthusianum*, or the Oregon black truffle. They are fruitier and softer in flavor than the first truffle I encountered, sweeter even, lending themselves to desserts as well as savory dishes. They are one of many ingredients used in an award-winning local amaro.

IN THE KITCHEN

Truffles are notoriously hard to describe as far as their flavor goes. Words like "earthy," "musky," "fruity," "cheesy," and the like have been used but fail miserably to capture the essence of what this ingredient is. I've tried for years to wax poetic about the effect this fungus has had on me personally, going so far as to describe how I've been deeply affected spiritually due to the taste of this strange tuber. But then I simply take a bite and realize I've failed and that I'm okay with it as long as I get to eat truffles.

Truffles, even our lesser-sought-after black truffle varieties, are very expensive and are not used to add bulk or heft to a dish but rather should be used sparingly and thought of more like a spice. They can be enjoyed raw, although they are susceptible to rot and should be inspected very carefully before using. Use a mandoline or microplane to shave truffles onto simple pastas like carbonara or linguine in a delicate cream sauce. They are lovely with eggs and garnish a patiently stirred risotto perfectly. They also infuse their fragrance into oils, butters, eggs, cheeses, and grains beautifully. Truffles need to be stored in the fridge in an airtight container to maintain freshness, so tuck them in alongside some dry rice or butter. Use the butter and rice to make the risotto, then finish with shaved fresh truffle. If you're not planning on making risotto, store truffles wrapped in paper towels to help remove the moisture from the fungi. Use them as quickly as you can as they break down rather fast.

Marasmius oreades

Fairy ring mushroom

FAMILY: Marasmiaceae

APPEARANCE: Smooth cap ranging in color from red-tinted tan to light brown or even white, depending on age. Gills are white or cream, shallow when young but wide-spaced as the mushroom matures.

HABITAT: Typically found in grass, usually in rings or arcs. Commonly in parks, lawns, and fields. They like to stay close to places populated with people.

SEASON: Spring, summer, and fall. Can be found in all seasons except when it gets quite cold.

THE TERM *MARASMIUS* COMES FROM the Greek word *marasmos* meaning "wasting away or withering." This name is in reference to the unique ability of this mushroom to dry out and then live on after a thorough soaking from rain, enough so that it continues to produce spores after rehydrating.

The common name, fairy ring, pertains to a circular formation of mushrooms that can encompass either a small cluster or expand to several feet in diameter annually. Fairy rings were once believed to be created by fairies, and while I love that story, I also love the science behind the rings. When a mushroom spore lands in a suitable spot, the underground hyphae spread out evenly in all directions. As the fungus grows, ages, and sucks up the nutrients from the soil, the center becomes what's known as a necrotic or dead zone in the shape of a circle. The fruiting bodies (a.k.a. mushrooms) emerge aboveground in a ring when it produces them. As the mushroom dies, the fungus lives on and can continue to fruit in the same spot, and even grow, for many years. *Marasmius oreades* is one of the best-known mushroom varieties that create these magical circles.

While it is often typical to come across little brown mushrooms (known fondly as LBMs) and stop there, because identification is so difficult, certain LBMs, such as the fairy ring mushroom, are worth getting to know in order to accurately recognize their species. You can often find them clustered, and they grow in the same spot year after year. They have a pleasant umami flavor and add heft and depth to soups, sauces, and stocks. It's important to note that they must be cooked as they are toxic when raw; they contain cyanohydrin, which helps the mushrooms keep the slugs away. Connect with an expert forager or your local mycological society to ensure proper identification as they can look very similar to nonedible species.

Morchella eximia, *sextelata,* and *exuberans*

Fire morels

FAMILY: Morchellaceae

APPEARANCE: Very similar in appearance to the black morel. They are dark gray-brown to black with ridges scattered vertically. The stem is generally creamy to pale yellow, although there is another type of fire morel, *Morchella tomentosa,* or the gray morel, that has a velvety dark gray or black stem.

HABITAT: Fire morels (*Morchella eximia, M. sextelata,* and *M. exuberans*) are all found in forests that have recently been burned. The biggest flush often is the year after, but some burns have produced these fungi a couple of years after the fire.

SEASON: Spring to early summer

THE QUEST FOR FIRE MORELS is one that often leaves you feeling like you are on another planet. Charred tree trunks leave a charcoal print on your clothes and hands. They feel light and fragile as you brush against them. Young green plants show signs of new life amid a barren scene and then, if you're lucky, you may also find fire morels. Starting with fire morels is a wise choice for beginning foragers. Online resources readily provide information about recent burns, essentially providing a hunting map. The foraging areas are typically quite bare, making it relatively easy to locate morels. Because of this ease, timing becomes crucial as other foragers are also in hot pursuit. Remember to harvest only what you will use and leave some for others to experience the same thrill. It's worth noting that elk appear to have an affinity for these morels, as I frequently come across signs of their presence near the mushrooms. I like to leave some for them and other beings that like the morels as much as I do.

The current science around this mushroom, like the morel itself, is still elusive. Many mushrooms have a mycorrhizal connection to certain trees and plants, but with morels we don't yet fully understand why they grow where they grow. We do know, however, that many varieties grow in abundance after wildfires. Morels tend to be among the first to usher in new life amid charred trees and a forest floor of ash.

Facing image (from left) *Morchella eximia,* *Morchella sextelata,* and *Morchella exuberans*

Morchella snyderi

Mountain black morel

FAMILY: Morchellaceae

APPEARANCE: The cap has a honeycomb-like texture which is completely hollow, as is the stem. When young, the cap is creamy white to pale yellow. As the mushroom matures, the cap turns dark gray-brown or black.

HABITAT: Natural morels are often found in the mountains several weeks after the snow melts. Some swear by the presence of the *Calypso* orchid around morels, but that's not always the case. They prefer the mountainous conifer forests filled with Douglas fir, ponderosa pine, and white fir.

SEASON: Late spring into early summer

AT FIRST GLANCE, THE MOREL looks like a crumpled-up piece of parchment paper, but upon closer inspection you'll find a unique and intricate structure that sets it apart from all other fungi: its honeycomb-like cap and stem make the morel quite easy to identify. Once the mushroom has been dissected, you'll see that the cap and stem are fused and hollow throughout. This key feature easily distinguishes the morel from two of its look-alikes, *Verpa bohemica* and *Gyromitra esculenta* (page 74).

Finding natural morel mushrooms can be significantly more challenging compared to searching for fire morels (page 102) because they are frequently discovered in dense forest environments with plenty of hiding spots. Morels are especially abundant in the spring, bringing a burst of flavor and excitement to the region after a typically long, dark winter. The soil needs to be well warmed, but it needs to be done gradually. Morels don't like a quick jump in temperature. When foraging for morels, you will quickly grow to loathe pine cones. If I had a nickel for every time I have squealed for joy at the sight of a "morel" only to discover that I've delighted over a pine cone, well, I'd have enough to buy a pound of morels in April at the grocery store, which can sometimes fetch a price of forty dollars or more.

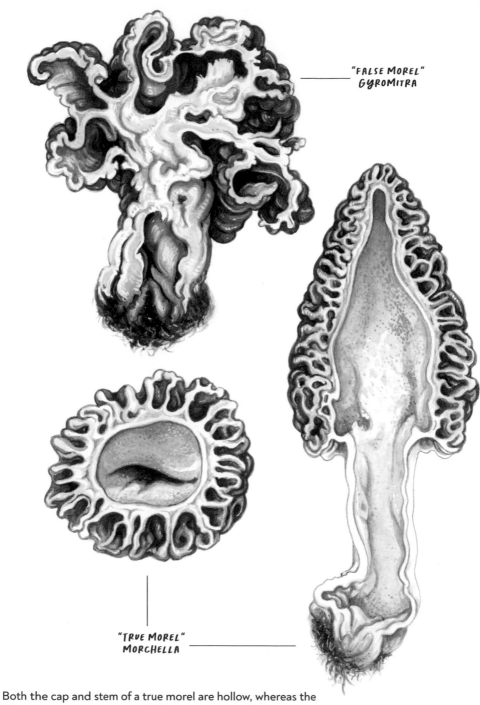

"FALSE MOREL"
GYROMITRA

"TRUE MOREL"
MORCHELLA

Both the cap and stem of a true morel are hollow, whereas the false morel is nearly solid and filled with cottony fibers.

IN THE KITCHEN

Some continue to debate the edibility of morels. It is widely known that they are toxic when raw, but even when cooked, a small percentage of people have reported allergic reactions. Germany's mycological society has thus removed the morel from the list of edible mushrooms. You wouldn't find Meriwether Lewis complaining of this news—he once described morels as "tasteless and insipid" after trying them on his journey out West with William Clark. But others, me included, would describe the taste of morels as being meaty, earthy, nutty, and even faintly reminiscent of the prized truffle (but that might just be me). These mushrooms are my top choice due to their delicious taste and delightful texture. You don't need many morels to enhance the flavor of a springtime dish.

Morels epitomize the adage "what grows together goes together." What's appearing in the garden and at the farmers' market when the morels are popping up in the woods makes the perfect pairing on the plate. Asparagus, peas, and morels make the best of friends. As do tender, sweet spring onions.

Morels dehydrate like a dream, extending their use in the kitchen all year long. Some even say that like fine wine, dried morels improve with time. Mine never last long enough to test that theory. Their robust flavor makes them a perfect candidate for a hearty mushroom powder that can be used to add umami to marinades, soups, sauces, and long braises. Every summer I make an all-purpose seasoning salt that I take on all our outdoor adventures, and it always includes a hefty portion of dried morels, along with herbs, citrus, and chilies.

Note that morels need to be thoroughly cooked before ingesting as they are toxic when raw.

Mycena haematopus

Bleeding fairy helmet

FAMILY: Mycenaceae

APPEARANCE: Oval or bell-shaped cap with scalloped edge. Ranges in color from pink to reddish brown. Thin stalk in muted brown-red, with milky deep-red latex that oozes from the stem and the cap.

HABITAT: Often found in groups on decaying logs and stumps of both hardwoods and conifers.

SEASON: Spring and fall

THIS MIGHT BE ONE OF the coolest, most unassuming mushrooms. The *Mycena* genus is large, but the mushrooms are small, so it's likely you've walked right past them. Of all the places they are found, they're most abundant in the Northwest. *Mycena haematopus*, otherwise known as bleeding fairy helmet or the blood-foot mushroom, is most widely recognized by the red latex that "bleeds" from the stem and the cap. The dainty caps, no larger than 1 to 4 cm across, have scalloped edges that are often light pink to brownish red in color. The stem is frequently a muted reddish-brown color, and the bleeding occurs when the tissue is cut or damaged, such as when plucked. The most bleeding will occur in young, fresh fruiting bodies. There is another type of *Mycena* that oozes, but unlike *Mycena haematopus*, *Mycena sanguinolenta* grows in soil, not decaying wood.

Nidula candida

Bird's nest fungi

FAMILY: Agaricaceae

APPEARANCE: Like a small bird's nest with tiny "eggs" inside a cup, around 3 to 8 mm, that is often gray or brown with a woolly covering around the exterior.

HABITAT: Usually found growing in woody soil debris, with small twigs and sticks.

SEASON: Most commonly found in the fall with the "eggs," or peridioles. The empty nests can be found throughout the year.

THESE STRANGE YET DELIGHTFUL FUNGI are so small that you have probably walked right past them without even noticing them. There are many bird's nest fungi varieties, but the *Nidula candida* is one of the most widespread species in our area. They look like, you guessed it, a bird's nest in miniature. They often grow on twigs laying on the forest floor. Inside the nest are tiny "eggs," called peridioles, which are little bundles that contain the spores. The cup shape of the bird's nest fungi is the perfect raindrop catcher. Rain falls into the cup and then out splashes the peridioles, spreading the spores. One single drop of rain has the power to shoot the spores up to seven feet away from the cup! They can also be spread by animals passing by who happen to disturb the nest, causing the peridioles to spill out (or be carried away with the animal). Once the spores are dispersed, the outer wall of the cup breaks down and decays or is consumed by insects.

Another type of bird's nest fungi found in the Northwest is the *Cyathus striatus*. They are similar in form, but their peridioles are attached by short cords. When a raindrop or other disturbance hits the nest, the peridioles are sent flying through the air, which signals the launch of these minuscule hyphae "ropes." These ropes are covered in a sticky mucilage that helps to adhere them to grass or another structure nearby while they wait for a hungry forest friend to come and eat said grass. The mushroom's spores are dispersed as the grass is passed, which is why you'll often find this variety growing in animal droppings.

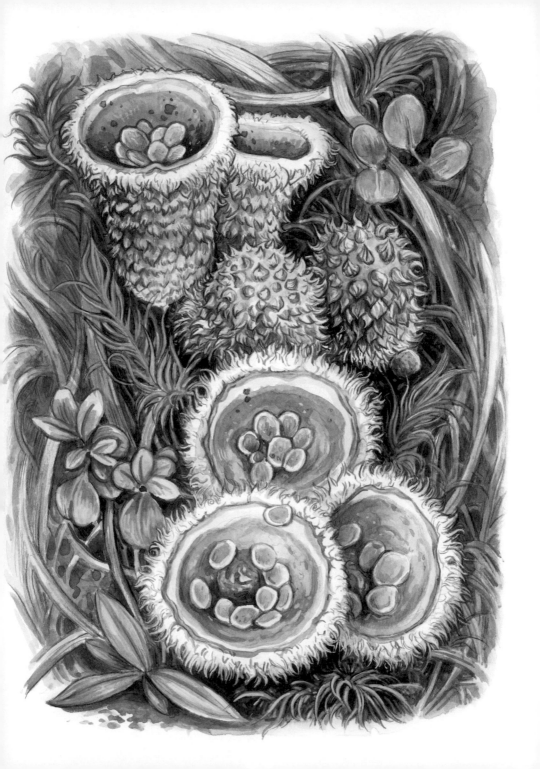

Omphalotus olearius

Jack o'lantern

FAMILY: Marasmiaceae

APPEARANCE: Bright yellow-gold to orange with olive tones. Bright yellow-orange decurrent gills. Luminescent when fresh.

HABITAT: Grows in clumps or groups on decaying wood, sometimes on buried deadwood.

SEASON: Summer through fall

KNOWN MOSTLY FOR TRICKING SOME foragers into thinking it is a chanterelle, *Omphalotus olearius,* or the jack o'lantern, is a lot more than just a poisonous look-alike. The bioluminescence of this mushroom makes it truly unique.

Bioluminescence refers to the emission of light by living organisms due to chemical reactions taking place within their bodies. Although glowing mushrooms have been studied for quite some time, it wasn't until 2015 that it was really understood why some mushrooms were bioluminescent. At that time, a team of researchers discovered that the mushrooms used their luciferins, which are the light-emitting compounds, to attract insects. These insects help spread the mushroom spores far and wide, helping to ensure the survival of the jack o'lantern.

They are most commonly found in California, but there have been reports of jack o'lantern sightings in Washington and Oregon. If you are foraging for chanterelles, it is important to understand how these two mushrooms are distinct from one another. First of all, the poisonous jack o'lanterns have true gills, whereas the gills of chanterelles are known as false gills. If you look closely, the false gills don't follow a linear pattern and have a forked ridge. (They aren't gills at all, but rather folds.) Jack o'lanterns are saprophytic, meaning they grow on and break down deadwood, so you'll find them growing on dead trees or on buried deadwood. Chanterelles are mycorrhizal, forming relationships with trees but growing directly in the dirt. Jack o'lanterns grow in large clusters, whereas chanterelles are often found singly or occasionally in small groupings.

Phaeolus schweinitzii

Dyer's polypore

FAMILY: Fomitopsidaceae

APPEARANCE: When young, color ranges from greenish to yellow and orange. It turns deep brown or grayish brown as it ages. It's soft and velvety in texture, growing in a platelike structure resembling rosettes.

HABITAT: Found at the base of conifer trees, either near the roots in the soil or on stumps and snags.

SEASON: Beginning of fall

PHAEOLUS SCHWEINITZII IS FOUND AT the base of conifer trees, which unfortunately means the tree on which this fungus is growing will eventually die. The mycelium from these fungi attack the roots and heartwood of its victim (or host), which causes decay.

Dyer's polypore is plush and velvety when young, with a yellow band running around the rim. It is most known for its use as a natural dye, producing a wide range of colors depending on the age of the mushroom and what mordant is used in the process. To use it as a dye, tear the mushroom into small pieces, about the size of a quarter. Add the pieces to a large pot of simmering water. The more mushrooms you use, the brighter the dye will be. Simmer for one hour, then add pre-mordanted yarn or other fibers to the pot. Simmer the fibers in the pot for at least fifteen minutes, or until you attain your desired color. The color of the fibers will lighten as they dry.

Phallus impudicus

Common stinkhorn

FAMILY: Phallaceae

APPEARANCE: Begins as a round egg with a white to white-yellow skin. The stalk elongates and pushes a spore-filled slimy headlike cap.

HABITAT: Favorable conditions include sandy coastal dunes, lawns, compost piles, wood shavings, and cultivated soils.

SEASON: Spring/summer

BEHOLD THE *PHALLUS IMPUDICUS* as it makes its grand and rapid entrance—a cheeky phallic shape, standing tall and quite unapologetic as the stem breaks free from the egg. Donning a slimy olive-green outfit, it matures into a full-grown stinkhorn, topping off the ensemble with a dark spore-packed cap. Besides the suggestive shape, another of the stinkhorn's distinctive features is a robust and offensive odor akin to decaying flesh that entices flies and insects as carriers of its spores via a putrid slime. This potent fragrance permeates the air, reaching far and wide. If you're lucky, you could stumble upon the stinkhorn in the woods, then literally watch it grow (from a distance so as not to be overwhelmed by the scent). This rapid growth adaptation allows the stinkhorn to disperse spores and attract insects while staying clear of predators.

Studies reveal the stinkhorn's medicinal prowess, containing anti-inflammatory compounds, while folklore tells of its use in treating gout, epilepsy, and breast cancer. Its pungent scent deters consumption, but the stem, once unveiled, offers a mild radish-like flavor. The egg, before the phallic shape and stench arise, can be consumed raw but I've yet to try it; instead, I regard this mushroom from a safe distance with admiration. (Unlike Etty, the eldest daughter of Charles Darwin, who had a peculiar habit of gathering and incinerating stinkhorns discovered on her property. She believed this rather unorthodox practice would safeguard the virtue of her maids, shielding them from any impure thoughts induced by the suggestive shape of the mushroom.)

Pleurocybella porrigens

Angel wing

FAMILY: Phyllotopsidaceae

APPEARANCE: Smooth white cap with a half-moon or fan shape. Sometimes you may notice a small stub, but generally there is no stem. The gills under the cap are generally white or off-white and tightly packed.

HABITAT: They grow in shelflike clusters on rotting old conifers, favoring hemlock.

SEASON: Late summer to mid-fall

EDIBLE OR NOT? THAT IS the hotly debated question around this mushroom. In 2004, over fifty instances of food poisoning, resulting in seventeen fatalities, were linked to the angel wing in Japan. It's important to note that all the victims were older in age and had a history of kidney problems. No other cases had been reported before this incident, and no deaths have been associated with this mushroom in North America. There are many who enjoy angel wing and experience no ill effects; however, I tend to stick with the *Pleurotus pulmonarius,* or oyster mushroom (pages 121–123). In fact, it was because of my desire to forage oysters that I learned how to identify angel wings as they have quite a few similarities.

Pleurocybella porrigens is typically found growing on conifer logs and stumps, particularly hemlock, here in the Northwest. It is a small, thin, white-fleshed fungi with a fanlike cap that projects out from the decaying wood it's growing on. These mushrooms have closely spaced white gills that are decurrent (running all the way down the fungi), with no stem. The key features that distinguish angel wings from oyster mushrooms are color, shape, and where they are growing. Oyster mushrooms are typically not bright white but grayer or lilac-tinged. Angel wings tend to have a more funneled shape, while all oysters look more like shells. Finally, oyster mushrooms are common on hardwoods like alder, whereas angel wings grow on conifers. You'll often find *Pleurocybella porrigens* growing scattered or in small clusters from late summer into fall. They tend to like dense, mossy woods, which makes their brilliant white color stand out in stark contrast to their surroundings, almost like, you guessed it, angel wings.

Pleurotus pulmonarius

Oyster mushroom

FAMILY: Pleurotaceae

APPEARANCE: Usually
grows in clusters in a
shelflike formation.
Stem is off-center and
sometimes hardly visible.
Large smooth cap, usually
cream, pinkish, or gray.
White or cream gills run
down to the stem.

HABITAT: Grows on
decaying alder.

SEASON: Grows in all sea-
sons if the temperatures
remain mild. Particularly
abundant in spring.

EXCUSE ME A MOMENT WHILE I absolutely gush about
oyster mushrooms. They are abundant, delicious, medicinal, and so incredibly fascinating. First, did you know
that this species of mushroom is not vegetarian and,
in fact, is a skilled hunter? It begins by weaving a net
using its mycelium. Unsuspecting nematodes digging
through deadwood get caught in this web. Meanwhile, the
Pleurotus moves on to the next phase of its attack. At the
tip of its hyphae is a droplet of toxic chemicals that par-
alyzes the nematodes. The hyphae then make their way
through the mouth and digest the worm from the inside
out. This process makes the oyster mushroom one of the
most protein-dense of all fungi. It is also loaded with
other essential nutrients like fiber, vitamins (including
vitamin B complex), and minerals (such as potassium and
iron) and offers a dose of powerful antioxidants. What's
more, these remarkable fungi contain special compounds
like lovastatin, known for its cholesterol-lowering effects,
and beta-glucans, which work wonders in boosting the
immune system. Ongoing studies explore their potential
in combating inflammation, fighting viruses, and even
combating cancer, though more research is required to
unlock their full therapeutic potential.

Oyster mushrooms could also be used as a major tool
to heal our planet. In his book *Entangled Life,* Merlin
Sheldrake writes about the power of *Pleurotus* mycelium
to break down our garbage, including dirty diapers.
(Oyster mushrooms are easy to cultivate and can grow
in a variety of substrates, as illustrated by these fruiting
bodies growing in abundance on diapers.)

The mushrooms were then tested and found healthy and free of any human diseases. This is just one example of using *Pleurotus* for what Paul Stamets calls mycoremediation, which is a method by which fungi may save the world by helping to restore damaged ecosystems. *Pleurotus* mycelium is also being used to create packaging as an alternative to Styrofoam that easily and quickly breaks down, adding nutrients back into the soil.

In the Northwest, *P. pulmonarius* are commonly found growing on dead alder in both the spring and fall. Another species, *P. populinus*, is often found on aspen and cottonwoods. I've found enough to fill my baskets in local natural areas around Seattle. They are also easily cultivated, and home-growing kits are readily available.

IN THE KITCHEN

Oyster mushrooms have a delicate, mild flavor with a subtle hint of seafood. Their texture is firm and meaty, and they easily soak up the flavors used in the dish. One of my favorite ways to use young, fresh, and firm oyster mushrooms is to batter them as you would an oyster, then fry until deeply browned and thoroughly crisp. Serve them on a roll with a bright rémoulade and thinly sliced lettuce plus plenty of hot sauce. Oyster mushrooms also dehydrate beautifully and rehydrate into a fragrant stock, or they can be sautéed and used in a variety of dishes. Often, I will use the dried mushrooms to turn into a mushroom powder that I add to seasoning salts or marinade, and even in my bread doughs and other baked goods to add a nutritional boost as well as a meaty depth of flavor. Typically, I'll add about a tablespoon of mushroom powder for every two cups of flour used in baked goods, but this can be easily modified.

Pseudohydnum gelatinosum

Cat's tongue

FAMILY: Tremellaceae

APPEARANCE: Fruiting body appears transluscent white to light gray. The cap is fan-shaped, with the underside showing soft teeth that hang. Stem is typically attached to the cap, although it can be found with just the cap attached to the substrate.

HABITAT: Grows alone or in groups on decaying woods, often found in Douglas fir forests.

SEASON: Late summer to winter

OTHERWISE KNOWN AS THE TOOTHED jelly fungus, jelly fungus, or cat's tongue, *Pseudohydnum gelatinosum* is an almost otherworldly looking species. The name *Pseudohydnum* refers to the fact that the teeth look similar to the *Hydnum* variety (hedgehog mushrooms) but aren't. It is those teeth that give this mushroom an appearance akin to a cat's tongue. Standing in stark contrast against the dark duff and decaying wood of the forest floor, this translucent mushroom looks like a little white woodland ghost.

Like many other jelly fungi, these are edible but lacking in flavor; they will, however, take on flavor if left to marinate. To make a sort of mushroom gummy candy, dehydrate the cat's tongue partially, then rehydrate by soaking the fungus in juice or other liquid. Just be aware that many compare their texture to rubber bands, so I tend to simply admire this strange and wonderful mushroom and leave it to linger in the woods.

Psilocybe semilanceata

Liberty cap

FAMILY:
Hymenogastraceae

APPEARANCE: Pointed cap typically brown or chestnut color on a thin stem with an often hard-to-spot ring. The stem and dark brown gills will start to bruise blue when handled.

HABITAT: Often found in disturbed pastures and tall grasses.

SEASON: Late summer through early winter

THE *PSILOCYBE SEMILANCEATA*, COMMONLY REFERRED to as the liberty cap, is one of the many fungi species in our region that contain psychoactive capabilities. These now-common species were once quite rare, but thanks to intrepid Johnny Appleseed–like individuals, patches of *Psilocybes* can now be found all over the Northwest. *Psilocybe semilanceata* is commonly found in damp grass west of the Cascades in fall to early winter. You can still find them growing in coastal regions of Washington and Oregon in the spring, but they are not as plentiful.

More and more research is being done on the dramatic effects psilocybin can have on those affected by anxiety and depression. In his book *How to Change Your Mind*, Michael Pollan speaks to some of the experiences the participants in these studies have: "Participants ranked their psilocybin experience as one of the most meaningful in their lives, comparable 'to the birth of a first child or death of a parent.' Two-thirds of the participants rated the session among the top five 'most spiritually significant experiences' of their lives; one-third ranked it the most significant such experience in their lives."

More individuals are opting for microdosing psilocybin, which involves taking small doses to derive its benefits while maintaining normal daily activities, rather than solely relying on a mind-altering trip. Currently, there is not a lot of scientific evidence for microdosing and the studies that are out now have mixed results regarding its efficacy. However, many people have reported that their symptoms from PTSD, anxiety, depression, ADHD, or chronic pain have lessened while microdosing. Others report that microdosing helps them boost both their creativity and mood.

As with all mushrooms, make sure you've identified them with 100 percent accuracy; psychedelic mushrooms are very hard to identify (and, of course, consumption of such mushrooms is federally illegal, although, as of the time of this writing, pathways to state decriminalization are underway in Washington and Oregon).

Ramaria botrytis

Pink-tipped coral

FAMILY: Gomphaceae

APPEARANCE: Large
white stem with branch-
ing patterns producing
pink tips when young
and fresh.

HABITAT: Grows in the soil
in conifer forests favoring
spruce and true fir.

SEASON: Fall

RAMARIA BOTRYTIS, OR PINK-TIPPED CORAL, is one species of over eighty different varieties in the *Ramaria* genus. Any of the coral mushrooms are a delight to come across in the woods; they give me the sense that I have been transported to the ocean floor. Many types can be enjoyed on the plate, and some can also be used in the dyer's pot, including *Ramaria botrytis.* The colors may be pale, but the best results come from using fresh mush-rooms, an iron mordant, and a dyebath that is basic (pH 9+). The resulting dye ranges from browns and tans to warm yellows.

The branching stemlike structures provide more sur-face area to release their spores in the same way that gills act on other mushroom types. The pink-tipped coral is the most commonly consumed coral, although I've not yet eaten any coral species. Instead, I simply delight in their charm and unique appearance, characterized by delicate pink hues transitioning to creamy white as you move from the upper branches to the stem. There are a few look-alikes, but the stems of *Ramaria botrytis* stain yellow or light brown.

Russula brevipes

Short-stemmed brittlegill

FAMILY: Russulaceae

APPEARANCE: Large, dry, white cap, concave and depressed when young. White gills under the cap that stop at the firm stem.

HABITAT: Grows alone or in groups in the soil of conifer and mixed forests. Typically found under mounds of soil and duff that are called shrumps or mushrumps.

SEASON: Fall into early winter

I'LL ADMIT THAT OFTEN MY excitement in finding this mushroom in the wild is because I'll likely encounter lobster mushrooms (*Hypomyces lactifluorum*, pages 83–85) nearby. But I include it here to give the short-stemmed brittlegill the attention it deserves and to challenge myself to get to know this mushroom better so that I can appreciate it for itself and not just for what the parasitized version offers. Poor *Russula brevipes:* David Arora goes so far as to say it is "better kicked than picked." It was the uncontested winner, receiving the most votes by far, of the "Most Boring Mushroom" in the eighth annual Santa Cruz Fungus Fair. I think it just needs better PR.

Its stunning white color and large cap make it easy to find when contrasting against dark, damp soil. From a distance, many mistake the shrump for a matsutake, which probably also lends to the disappointment when one realizes it's just a *Russula brevipes*. The cap is depressed—probably because no one appreciates it (sorry, I couldn't help myself). The stem is quite hard, and the flesh is crisp. It is edible but best used to add bulk rather than flavor. (Hmm, not sure if I did this mushroom any favors.)

Sparassis radicata

Cauliflower mushroom

FAMILY: Sparassidaceae

APPEARANCE: Creamy, pale-white or yellowish tan in color. Attached via a single base or stalk to the roots of old conifers.

HABITAT: Typically grows at the base or on the roots of trees and seems to enjoy Douglas fir and other pine-family members.

SEASON: Fall through early winter

DURING ONE OF MY WOODLAND adventures I had a delightful encounter with this somewhat-rare mushroom. My companion stumbled upon it, but it was past its prime, so I didn't have the chance to savor it for dinner. But I was still absolutely thrilled just to lay my eyes on this remarkable species. *Sparassis radicata,* also known as the cauliflower mushroom or brain mushroom, is a unique fungus with a distinct appearance. Its fruiting body is large and ruffled, resembling a cauliflower head or a convoluted brain. What you see growing is actually the blossoming fruit of a thin stalk that can extend up to six feet underground.

This is an edible mushroom that lends itself to your culinary creativity as it really is all about that noodly texture. The mushroom itself soaks up whatever flavors it mingles with, but stays firm like an al dente noodle. The fact that it is a polypore, a characteristically woody group of mushrooms, explains its sturdiness.

Trametes versicolor

Turkey tail

FAMILY: Polyporaceae

APPEARANCE: Leathery cap with concentric arcs of contrasting colors in tones of brown, red, white, gray, purple, and sometimes greenish blue. Underside is generally creamy-white when young and has tiny pores.

HABITAT: Grows in shelf-like groupings on dead hardwood.

SEASON: Throughout the year but abundant in winter to early spring

TRAMETES VERSICOLOR IS A TRULY remarkable mushroom that grows abundantly, has an eye-catching appearance, and while it's too hard to cook with, it can be processed to unlock a wealth of medicinal properties. When I venture out foraging, it never fails to catch my attention and earn a place in my mushroom basket. Its captivating display of muted rainbowlike colors forms a beautiful fan shape, typically growing on decaying hardwood, with a special affinity for alders, oaks, and fruit trees. Turkey tail mushrooms belong to the bracket fungus family and feature tubelike pores with a velvety texture on top that feels remarkably soft, reminiscent of suede.

For centuries, turkey tail has been recognized for its potent medicinal properties. It is renowned for combating fatigue, supporting gut health, bolstering the immune system, and effectively fighting off harmful pathogens. In fact, it stands out as one of the most extensively researched mushrooms worldwide. Mycologist Paul Stamets claims that turkey tail is one of the fungi with the most antiviral activity. The others on that list include agarikon (*Laricifomes officinalis*), chaga (*Inonotus obliquus*), reishi (*Ganoderma* spp., page 69), and birch polypore (*Fomitopsis betulina*). One of the key components responsible for its immune-supporting benefits is a group of compounds called beta-glucans. Ingesting these beta-glucans can be likened to powerlifting for the immune system, as they support and prime the body to effectively combat potential threats.

In his wildly popular TED Talk, Paul Stamets tells the story of how he believes turkey tail mushrooms helped heal his eighty-five-year-old mother of breast cancer. I have seen his talk and the documentary *Fantastic Fungi*, in which he also tells this story many times. At the end of the TED Talk he brings his healed mother up onto the stage and they tearily embrace. Each time I watch it, I also tear up and marvel at the wonders of this potent medicinal mushroom.

HOW TO MAKE A TURKEY TAIL TINCTURE OR TEA

When it comes to extracting this mushroom's beneficial compounds, alcohol extracts have shown the most promise thus far. These extracts offer a concentrated form that maximizes the potential health benefits of the mushroom.

Clean your mushrooms with a damp cloth, or brush any soil and debris off with a mushroom brush or other food-safe brush.

Dehydrate the turkey tail mushrooms until brittle. Use a dehydrator, or place the mushrooms in a single layer on a sheet pan, then heat in the oven on the lowest setting, around 170 degrees F, for up to a few hours. Once they snap when you squeeze or try to bend them, transfer the mushrooms to a food processor or grinder, and grind into a fine, fluffy powder. Grinding the mushrooms into a fine powder creates more surface area for an extraction, which will give you the most medicinal potency.

Weigh the powder. For every ounce, add 5 ounces of alcohol to the jar. Most plants and mushrooms are extracted best with a 40–60 percent alcohol.

Let this sit for four to six weeks, then strain using a fine-mesh strainer lined with muslin or cheesecloth.

Pour this mixture into a dark bottle with a dropper lid. Add a dropper full to tea, coffee, or other hot liquids, which will evaporate the alcohol and dilute the flavor.

You can also get some of the medicinal benefits from turkey tail by simmering the powder in water to make a tea. To make a potent water-based extract, add 1 ounce of ground mushrooms to 10 ounces of water. Simmer for twenty minutes, then let the mushrooms cool in the water. Strain through a cheesecloth. Refrigerate for up to a month, or freeze for up to a year. Freeze the extract in ice-cube trays and add a cube to stocks or soup, or simply thaw and drink for a medicinal boost. The dehydrated and ground mushrooms could be added to capsules and taken that way, but the medicinal properties are best extracted through water or alcohol.

Tricholoma murrillianum

Matsutake

THE WESTERN MATSUTAKE IS HIGHLY valued for its aromatic fragrance, often described as a mix of spicy cinnamon and pine, or as my friends Langdon Cook and Jon Rowley once taught me, like "Red Hots and dirty socks." This distinctive scent, oddly enough, makes it a sought-after ingredient in culinary dishes. *Matsutake* translates to "pine mushroom" in Japanese, and in Japan, where it is wildly popular, it fetches a price of up to $1,000 per pound.

Some people have confused other toxic *Amanita* varieties with the matsutake, but that sweet cinnamon candy scent is quite unmistakable. In case you need help remembering, Daniel Winkler uses the moniker "Missing the *matsi* aroma might induce kidney coma." You can also test the stem if you're in doubt. The stem of a matsutake is firm enough to stand up to some squeezing, but an *Amanita* will crumble. The thick veil is another distinguishing factor of this variety. It tends to prefer higher elevations and is commonly associated with coniferous forests. Matsutake are mycorrhizal and can be found in various habitats from coastal pine forests to mountain coniferous forests. Fruiting can happen from the first rains of fall all the way to the first frost.

Due to its popularity in the culinary world and its limited distribution, the western matsutake faces increasing pressure from overharvesting and habitat loss. Conservation efforts have been initiated to protect this species and ensure its sustainability. So if you do come across matsutake while foraging, be mindful and leave some for other foragers, human and other than human.

Tuber gibbosum and *oregonense*

Oregon white truffle

FAMILY: Tuberaceae

APPEARANCE: Round and knobby. The white truffle varieties are smaller than the black ones and range from peanut-size to about the diameter of a quarter. They are white to pale orangish-brown on the outside (once the dirt is washed off) and are marbled white and brown on the interior.

HABITAT: Found with Douglas firs west of the Cascades.

SEASON: Fall through spring, depending on the species

TUBER GIBBOSUM AND *TUBER OREGONENSE*, or Oregon white truffles, are very closely related to the famous European varieties, and in fact, these are some of the most well-known truffles on Earth (see also *Leucangium carthusianum*, page 95–97). Fruiting underground keeps this fungi protected from the elements and extreme temperatures. Their fruiting bodies are essentially folded over themselves, containing the spores within. In order for their spores to be released, these organisms depend on the inquisitiveness and appetite of neighboring animals. The potent fragrance emitted by the truffles lures in the hungry creatures, prompting them to unearth the truffles, indulge in a feast, and subsequently scatter the spores to other locations.

To locate and harvest these truffles, we often depend on the curiosity and the keen sense of smell of other animals. While some foragers use their understanding of mycorrhizal connections to comb the forest floor with a rake, this method can significantly disrupt the forest floor. Instead, I'd encourage you to opt for the assistance of trained dogs to sniff out the truffles. This approach is far less intrusive, and there's a unique joy in following a dog through the woods as it's drawn in by the alluring aroma. Fruiting season for the white truffles depends on the species. *Tuber gibbosum* typically fruits between January through June whereas *Tuber oregonense* is more likely found October through February.

Xerocomellus atropurpureus

Deep purple bolete

FAMILY: Boletaceae

APPEARANCE: Small to medium-sized mushroom with a dark purple-brown cap. It has a yellowish stem that is streaked with red connecting to a spongy yellow pore layer.

HABITAT: Found in conifer forests from the coast to the Cascades.

SEASON: Late summer into late fall

WHEN I FIRST CAME TO know this mushroom, it was introduced by the name Zeller's bolete. DNA testing has now revealed that Zeller's bolete is quite rare, and what we actually found were likely *Xerocomellus atropurpureus*, commonly known as the purple bolete. This is a species of edible mushroom belonging to the Boletaceae family and known for its distinctive dark purple to purplish-brown cap and yellow pores. These mushrooms grow in association with Douglas fir, but you'll have to look closely as the dark cap hides itself well amid the ferns and Oregon grape it often fruits around.

I'm a bit ashamed to admit that my first time finding this mushroom I was disappointed that our basket was not full of the chanterelles that I was really after on that early November forage. I was a novice then and mainly interested in the few wild edible species I knew of, but luckily, Daniel Winkler was my guide for that excursion, and he opened up a whole world of foraged foods outside the few I knew. One of those varieties was this deep purple bolete. We brought these back to the campsite, where I sautéed them in olive oil and garlic and used them to top a fire-cooked pizza with fresh mozzarella, chili, and arugula.

Acknowledgments

TO DANIEL WINKLER, LANGDON COOK, JON ROWLEY, Alana McGee, Rachel Zoller, and others who know much more about mushrooms than I do and yet they've taken me, an overeager learner and passionate pleader, into the woods with them. I owe them and many other mycologists and fungi lovers much gratitude for stirring the fungal excitement in me. This enthusiasm for mushrooms has changed my life.

Thank you to the entire team at Sasquatch: Hannah Elnan, Isabella Hardie, and Anna Goldstein. I'm so grateful that you all trusted me with this project and let me share my excitement (some may say obsession) for fungi.

Thank you Libby England for bringing these mushrooms to life.

To my kids, for joining me on many adventures even when you didn't always want to.

To my husband, for being my favorite adventure buddy.

To the Earth, my favorite teacher, guide, and friend.

Glossary

ANNULUS: The leftover ring on the stem from the remnants of a torn partial veil.

AREOLAE: The cracks that appear on some mushroom caps that form as the mushroom grows and the cap stretches.

BULBOUS: The swollen base at the bottom of the stem.

CAP/PILEUS: The structure on top of the mushroom that holds gills or pores.

GILLS/LAMELLA: Thin, papery structures tucked under the caps and down the stems of many mushroom varieties. The gills are used as a means to disperse spores and are a key factor in identifying different types of fungi.

GLEBA: The inner mass of certain fungi such as the puffball that contains the spores.

HYPHA: The branching threads (hyphae) or filaments that make up mycelium. A network of hyphae make up the body of a fungus, which is called the mycelium.

MARGIN: The edge of the cap.

MYCELIUM: The bulk of the fungus mass that consists of fine threadlike filaments called hyphae, which grow in the substrate where the fungus lives. The fungus uses the mycelium for digestion and absorption of water and nutrients and to connect to other plants and trees.

MYCOREMEDIATION: A term coined by Paul Stamets referring to the idea that mycelium can be selected and trained to break down toxic waste. It is a form of bioremediation in which fungi are used.

MYCORESTORATION: A term coined by Paul Stamets concerning the use of fungi to improve the health of the environment. Examples of this include filtering water through mycelium, helping trees to grow in forests and plants to grow in gardens.

MYCORRHIZAL: A symbiotic relationship of a fungus with certain plants.

PARASITIC: Fungi that can infect a living host and obtain nutrients, often causing harm to the host's function and structure.

PARTIAL VEIL: Tissue that extends from the stem to the edge of the cap when the mushroom is young. As the fruiting body ages, the veil disintegrates, leaving behind a ring that is commonly used for identification between species.

PORES: A structure found on some mushroom species that is used for spore dispersal. Pores appear as holes but are actually the ends of tubes held within the mushroom cap.

RETICULAE: The netted overlay of tissue located on the stems of many boletes such as Porcini.

SAPROBES: A group of fungi that work to break down dead or decaying plant matter. They are one of nature's great decomposers.

SHRUMP: Occasionally dubbed a "mushshrump," this term describes a bump in the ground where a mushroom is developing. It serves as a clue, particularly for species such as porcini (pages 38–41) or the lobster mushroom (pages 83–85), suggesting the presence of a hidden mushroom beneath an unassuming mound of soil.

SPORES: A cell used for reproduction. Fungal spores contain the mushroom's genetic material.

STRIATIONS: The wrinkled patterns that appear on the edge of the cap on some mushroom varieties.

TEETH: In the context of mushrooms, the word "teeth" is used to describe the spore-bearing structures on some mushrooms that can look like shaggy growths, spines, or thin branches. The teeth of a mushroom can be anywhere from a few millimeters to a few centimeters long.

UMBO: The raised center present on some mushroom caps.

UNIVERSAL VEIL: Thin tissue that fully covers young fruiting bodies of certain types of mushrooms. An example of this is the *Amanita muscaria* (page 28), where the white warts on the cap are the visible remnants of the universal veil.

VOLVA: The remnant of the universal veil that sits as a cuplike structure at the base of the mushroom.

WARTS: Pieces of the universal veil that is left on the cap.

ZONATIONS: Refers to different areas or zones that have different colors or textures on certain mushroom varieties.

Resources

Books on Mushrooms

Arora, David. *Mushrooms Demystified*. California: Ten Speed Press, 1986.

Arora, David. *All That the Rain Promises and More: A Hip Pocket Guide to Western Mushrooms*. California: Ten Speed Press, 1991.

Borsato, Diane. *Mushrooming: An Illustrated Guide to the Fantastic, Delicious, Deadly, and Strange World of Fungi*. New York: The Experiment, 2023.

Cage, John. *John Cage: A Mycological Foray: Variations on Mushrooms*. California: Atelier Éditions, 2020.

Millman, Lawrence. *Fungipedia: A Brief Compendium of Mushroom Lore*. New Jersey: Princeton University Press, 2019.

Sheldrake, Merlin. *Entangled Life: How Fungi Make Our Worlds, Change Our Minds, and Shape Our Futures*. New York: Random House, 2020.

Stamets, Paul. *Psilocybin Mushrooms of the World: An Identification Guide*. California: Ten Speed Press, 1996.

Stamets, Paul. *Mycelium Running: How Mushrooms Can Help Save the World*. California: Ten Speed Press, 2005.

Trudell, Steve. *Mushrooms of the Pacific Northwest: Revised Edition*. Oregon: Timber Press, 2022.

Whiteley, Aliya. *The Secret Life of Fungi: Discoveries from a Hidden World*. New York: Pegasus Books, 2022.

Winkler, David. *Fruits of the Forest: A Field Guide to Pacific Northwest Edible Mushrooms*. Washington: Mountaineers Books, 2022.

Other Fungi Resources

Bureau of Land Management
blm.gov

Cascade Mycological Society
cascademyco.org

Duwamish Tribe
duwamishtribe.org

Fantastic Fungi. Directed by Louie Schwartzberg, written by Mark Monroe, with performances by Paul Stamets, Michael Pollan, Eugenia Bone, Andrew Weil, Giuliana Furci, et al., Moving Art, 2019.

Forest Service (information on permitting for foraging)
fs.usda.gov

International Mushroom Dye Institute
mushroomsforcolor.com

Learn Your Land, YouTube series
learnyourland.com

Muckleshoot Tribe
muckleshoot.nsn.us

MushroomExpert.com

Mushroom Color Atlas
mushroomcoloratlas.com

Northwest Mushroomers Society
  northwestmushroomers.org

Oregon Mycological Society
  wildmushrooms.org

PaulStamets.com

Puget Sound Mycological Society
  psms.org

Snohomish County Mycological Society
  scmsfungi.org

Snoqualmie Tribe
  snoqualmietribe.us

South Sound Mushroom Club
  southsoundmushroomclub.com

South Vancouver Island Mycological Society
  svims.club

Southwest Washington Mycological Society
  swmushrooms.org

Suquamish Tribe
  suquamish.nsn.us

Vancouver Mycological Society
  vanmyco.org

Washington State Department of Natural Resources
  dnr.wa.gov

Willamette Valley Mushroom Society
  https://www.wvmssalem.org

Yakima Valley Mushroom Society
  https://yvms.org

Yellow Elanor, YouTube series & @yellowelanor on
  Instagram: yellowelanor.com

Index

Page numbers in *italics* refer to illustrations.

A

Agaricaceae
Agaricus augustus, *24–25*
Calvatia sculpta, *42–43*
Coprinus comatus, 52–55, *54, 55*
Nidula candida, 110–*11*
Agaricus augustus, *24–25*
Aleuria aurantia, *26–27*
Amanita muscaria, 28–29, 39
Amanita phalloides, *30*–31
Amanitaceae
Amanita muscaria, *28–29*
Amanita phalloides, *30–31*
angel wing. See *Pleurocybella porrigens*
Armillaria ostoyae, *32–35*
artist's conk. See *Ganoderma applanatum*
Auricularia americana, *36–37*
Auriculariaceae. See *Auricularia americana*

B

Bankeraceae. See *Hydnellum peckii*
bear's head. See *Hericium abietis*
beefsteak polypore. See *Fistulina hepatica*
bird's nest fungi. See *Nidula candida*
black trumpet. See *Craterellus calicornucopioides*
bleeding fairy helmet. See *Mycena haematopus*
bleeding tooth. See *Hydnellum peckii*
blue-stain fungus. See *Chlorociboria aeruginascens*

Boletaceae
Boletus edulis, 38–41, *40–41*
Xerocomellus atropurpureus, 146–47
Boletus edulis, 38–41, *40–41*

C

Calvatia sculpta, *42–43*
candy cap. See *Lactarius rubidus*
Cantharellaceae
Cantharellus formosus, 44–47, *45, 47*
Cantharellus subalbidus, *48–49*
Craterellus calicornucopioides, *56–57*
Craterellus tubaeformis, *58–59*
Cantharellus formosus, 44–47, *45, 47*
Cantharellus subalbidus, *48–49*
cap, mushroom
candy cap. See *Lactarius rubidus*
death cap mushroom. See *Amanita phalloides*
liberty cap. See *Psilocybe semilanceata*
cat's tongue. See *Pseudohydnum gelatinosum*
cauliflower mushroom. See *Sparassis radicata*
chanterelle, mushroom
golden chanterelle. See *Cantharellus formosus*
white chanterelle. See *Cantharellus subalbidus*
winter chanterelle. See *Craterellus tubaeformis*
chicken of the woods. See *Laetiporus conifericola*
Chlorociboria aeruginascens, *50–51*
Chlorociboriaceae. See *Chlorociboria aeruginascens*

common stinkhorn. See *Phallus impudicus*

Cook, Langdon, 143

Coprinus comatus, 52–55, *54*, *55*

Craterellus calicornucopioides, 56–57

Craterellus tubaeformis, 58–59

Cyathus striatus, 110

D

Dacrymyces chrysospermus, 60–61

Dacrymycetaceae. See *Dacrymyces chrysospermus*, 60–61

dark honey fungus. See *Armillaria ostoyae*

death cap mushroom. See *Amanita phalloides*

deep purple bolete. See *Xerocomellus atropurpureus*

Discinaceae. See *Gyromitra esculenta*, 74–75

Dyer's polypore. See *Phaeolus schweinitzii*

E

earthstar. See *Geastrum saccatum*

F

fairy ring mushroom. See *Marasmius oreades*

fall, mushrooms during

Aleuria aurantia, 26–27

Amanita muscaria, 28–29

Amanita phalloides

Amanita phalloides, 30–31

Boletus edulis, 38–41, *40–41*

Cantharellus subalbidus, 48–*49*

Craterellus tubaeformis, 58–*59*

Fistulina hepatica, 62–*63*

Geastrum saccatum, 70–*71*

Lepista nuda, 92–*93*

Leucangium carthusianum, 94–97, *94*

Ramaria botrytis, *130*–31

Russula brevipes, *132–33*

Sparassis radicata, *134–35*

Tricholoma murrillianum, *142–43*

Tuber gibbosum, *144–45*

false morel. See *Gyromitra esculenta*

fire morel. See *Morchella eximia*

Fistulina hepatica, 62–63

Fistulinaceae. See *Fistulina hepatica*, 62–*63*

fly agaric. See *Amanita muscaria*

Fomitopsidaceae

Fomitopsis mounceae, 64–65

Laetiporus conifericola, 88, 88–91

Phaeolus schweinitzii, 114–*15*

Fomitopsis mounceae, 64–65

foraging, 16–19

fungi. *See* mushrooms

G

Ganoderma applanatum, 66–67

Ganoderma oregonense, 68–69

Ganodermataceae

Ganoderma applanatum, 66–67

Ganoderma oregonense, 68–69

Geastraceae. See *Geastrum saccatum*, 70–71

Geastrum saccatum, 70–71

golden chanterelle. See *Cantharellus formosus*

Gomphaceae

Gomphus clavatus, 72–73

Ramaria botrytis, *130*–31

Gomphus clavatus, 72–73

Gyromitra esculenta, 74–75

H

Hardman, Isabel, 50

Hericiaceae. See *Hericium abietis*

Hericium abietis, 76–79, *78–79*

Hydnellum peckii, 80–81

Hymenogastraceae. See *Psilocybe semilanceata*

Hypocreaceae. See *Hypomyces lactifluorum*

Hypomyces lactifluorum, 82–83

About the Author and Illustrator

ASHLEY RODRIGUEZ is a Seattle-based author, cooking instructor, food photographer, writer, partner, and mother of three children. She is the co-creator and host of James Beard Award–nominated outdoor-cooking-adventure series *Kitchen Unnecessary* and the top food blog *Not Without Salt*. She is also the author of three cookbooks and is a certified nature and forest therapy guide. When not eating (or talking and writing about food), Ashley loves to be foraging, fly-fishing, or hunting and spending as much time outside as possible.

LIBBY ENGLAND is a painter with a reverence for the divine in nature, seeking communion with both the spiritual and material worlds. Through her meticulous illustrations with an attentive focus on scientific accuracy, England often combines mythological, dreamlike, and mystical concepts in otherwise naturalistic scenes and landscapes. While closely examining the beauty of our environment, she opens portals to the numinous realms of humanity, exploring such perennial themes as life, death, suffering, and peace. She works out of her small cabin studio in the deep oak forests of East Texas with a cup of tea and her geriatric cat by her side.

Printed in China

SASQUATCH BOOKS with colophon is a registered trademark of Penguin Random House LLC

28 27 26 25 24   9 8 7 6 5 4 3 2 1

Illustrations: Libby England
Editor: Hannah Elnan
Production editor: Isabella Hardie
Designer: Anna Goldstein

Library of Congress Cataloging-in-Publication Data
Names: Rodriguez, Ashley, author | England, Elizabeth, illustrator
Title: Field notes from a fungi forager : an illustrated journey through the world of Pacific Northwest mushrooms / Ashley Rodriguez with illustrations by Libby England
Other titles: Illustrated journey through the world of Pacific Northwest mushrooms
Identifiers: LCCN 2023050574 (print) | LCCN 2023050575 (ebook) | ISBN 9781632175366 (hardcover) | ISBN 9781632175373 (ebook)
Subjects: LCSH: Mushrooms--Northwest, Pacific--Identification. | Mushrooms--Northwest, Pacific--Pictorial works. | Wild plants, Edible--Northwest, Pacific--Identification. | Field guides.
Classification: LCC QK605.5.N87 .R56 2024 (print) | LCC QK605.5.N87 (ebook) | DDC 579.609795--dc23/eng/20240207
LC record available at https://lccn.loc.gov/2023050574
LC ebook record available at https://lccn.loc.gov/2023050575

ISBN: 978-1-63217-536-6

Sasquatch Books
1325 Fourth Avenue, Suite 1025
Seattle, WA 98101

SasquatchBooks.com